Searching for
Sacred Ground

The C. Henry Smith series is edited by J. Denny Weaver. As is expected to be true of many future books in the CHS series, volumes published to date are being released by Cascadia Publishing House (originally Pandora Press U.S., a name some of the earlier series books carry) and copublished by Herald Press in cooperation with Bluffton University as well as the Mennonite Historical Society. Bluffton University, in consultation with the publishers, is primarily responsible for the content of the studies.

Searching for
Sacred Ground

The Journey of
Chief Lawrence Hart,
Mennonite

for Naomi —

Raylene Hinz-Penner

Foreword by Donald L. Fixico

Raylene Hinz-Penner

C. Henry Smith

The C. Henry Smith Series

Volume 7

Cascadia

Publishing House
Telford, Pennsylvania

copublished with
Herald Press
Scottdale, Pennsylvania

Cascadia Publishing House orders, information, reprint permissions:
contact@CascadiaPublishingHouse.com
1-215-723-9125
126 Klingerman Road, Telford PA 18969
www.CascadiaPublishingHouse.com

Searching for Sacred Ground
Copyright © 2007 by Cascadia Publishing House,
Telford, PA 18969
All rights reserved.
Copublished with Herald Press, Scottdale, PA
Library of Congress Catalog Number: 2006027650
ISBN-13: 978-1-931038-40-9; **ISBN 10**: 1-931038-40-6
Book design by Cascadia Publishing House
Cover design by Gwen M. Stamm

The paper used in this publication is recycled and meets the
minimum requirements of American National Standard for Information
Sciences—Permanence of Paper for Printed Library Materials, ANSI Z39.48-1984.

Grateful acknowledgment is made to the Lawrence and Betty Hart photo collection for
permission to use the cover photo, by Cyrus McCrimmon, *Rocky Mountain News.*

Library of Congress Cataloguing-in-Publication Data
Hinz-Penner, Raylene.
 Searching for sacred ground : the journey of Chief Lawrence Hart, Mennonite /
Raylene Hinz-Penner.
  p. cm. -- (C. Henry Smith series ; 7)
 Includes bibliographical references and index.
 ISBN-13: 978-1-931038-40-9 (6 x 9" trade pbk. : alk. paper)
 ISBN-10: 1-931038-40-6 (6 x 9" trade pbk. : alk. paper)
 1. Hart, Lawrence H. 2. Cheyenne Indians--Kings and rulers--Biography. 3. Men-
nonites--Oklahoma--Biography. 4. Cheyenne Indians--Missions--Oklahoma. 5.
Mennonites--Missions--Oklahoma. 6. Washita Campaign, 1868-1869--History. 7.
Oklahoma--Ethnic relations. I. Title. II. Series.

E99.C53H5 2007
289.7092--dc22
[B]

                                                                    2006027650

   16 15 14 13 12 11 10 09 08 07   10 9 8 7 6 5 4 3 2 1

CONTENTS

FOREWORD

Throughout history American Indian leaders have led their people during war and victory and defeat, famine, disease, removal, even surrender—all that has meant survival for their people, sometimes resulting in their own deaths. Being an Indian leader is strenuous and calls for generosity of time and energy. Such a role is not one so enviable or self-serving. To be an Indian leader is to serve one's people, community, and tribe. That is what this important book is about.

Lawrence Hart has dedicated his life to helping his people and others toward a better life and true understanding of it in the Cheyenne way. To be Cheyenne and a Cheyenne leader calls for commitment as well as the constant understanding and continuous support of one's family. Hart walks this road. As both a peace chief of the Cheyenne and a minister among Mennonites, Hart is two people in one and more.

In this insightful book, Raylene Hinz-Penner tells a beautiful story of a modern-day tribal leader who is part of living tradition and depended on by many for wisdom and moral strength. Indian leaders are like this: stalwarts of community, keepers of tradition, defenders for justice, and servants of their people. Their lives are not easy, as this volume shows, telling of Hart's challenges and triumphs—including being raised for his first six years in the Cheyenne language and ways by his grandparents, being educated in a boarding school, attending Bethel College, falling in love with future wife Betty, and becoming a Navy fighter pilot.

Hart's strength is his personal fortitude and grounding in the tradition of the Cheyenne past that he brings to the present. Lawrence walks the balanced path between conflict and peace, tradition and contemporary life, as he teaches others about being Cheyenne. His road is more complex for his acceptance of Christianity and becoming a Mennonite minister. In him are two beliefs—the Mennonite way and the Cheyenne way. Both stress the importance of living in peace with all things.

In the following pages, past and present are one reality as the author weaves tradition and modernity, telling about Black Kettle, the great peace chief in Cheyenne history, White Antelope, and others, and of how they live in Chief Hart. The story is a personal one yet intended to publicly introduce a special person. Hinz-Penner respectfully shares her insights about Hart's life as she describes his great reverence for leaders now gone yet still there for him in spirit.

The Cheyenne are a magnificent people whose presence on the Great Plains numbered several thousand souls during the mid-nineteenth century. The Cheyenne Council of Forty-Four governed their ten bands when they met annually to hold the Sun Dance and formally made final decisions that affected all Cheyenne. One decision was to always call the Arapahoes friends. Great warriors of various military societies and keepers of peace maintained the balance for a good life, yet this was not always easy for the Cheyenne and Arapahoe. This called for such grand leaders of war as Little Chief, Little Wolf, and Dull Knife— and of peace in the persons of Black Kettle and White Antelope. This list of leaders includes Bull Bear, Standing-in-Water, War Bonnet, Yellow Wolf, Knock Knee, One Eye, and John Woodenlegs. Their beliefs in tradition involving the Sacred Arrows, the Sacred Buffalo Hat, and Maheo, "Creator of All Things," defined their native ethos. This was the Cheyenne way. It is this Cheyenne leadership tradition to which Hart belongs—one of dignity, quiet strength, wisdom, and inclusive concern.

Hart is a modern-day peace chief and spiritual person who lives for his people guided by Cheyenne and Mennonite traditions. How is this possible? Hinz-Penner's moving words invite us to learn how by making us feel we are journeying with Hart in his sacred roles.

In my thirty years as a Native scholar, I have rarely read a biography that so reveals the powerful presence of traditionalism in a historical figure who still works in the present. For anyone wanting to know about the unparalleled challenges facing American Indian leaders today, Raylene Hinz-Penner has delivered a personalized biography that introduces one of the most incredible people readers will ever meet.

—*Donald L. Fixico, (Shawnee, Sac & Fox, Creek, Seminole)*
   Distinguished Foundation Professor of History, Arizona State University

SERIES PREFACE

C. Henry Smith began his teaching career at Goshen College, 1903-13, and then taught history at Bluffton College (now Bluffton University) from 1913-48, except for the 1922-23 year he spent at Bethel College. The first Mennonite in North America to earn a Ph.D. and remain in the Mennonite church, Smith was the premier North American Mennonite historian of his era. He wrote many articles for Mennonite periodicals and was a central figure in planning the *Mennonite Encyclopedia*. He published five major works over thirty-five years, more full-length writings than any other Mennonite historian of his time. Also a church leader, Smith was on the publication board of the General Conference Mennonite Church and the Peace Committee of Middle District.

Producing the C. Henry Smith Series (CHS) with cosponsorship of the Mennonite Historical Society is one dimension of the service Bluffton University seeks to provide the Mennonite church as well as Anabaptists at large and the wider Christian tradition. Smith's historical expertise, commitment to pacifism and nonresistance, commitment to the church, and wide-ranging interests beyond the discipline of history all represent the values and interests that characterize the series bearing his name. Naming the series for an individual of multiple interests and talents signals a vision to publish works that use a variety of disciplines and modes of inquiry to serve Anabaptist and Mennonite churches.

Works in the CHS Series reflect the assumption that a peace church worldview holds potential to shape discussion of any issue. These books present no consensus view, however, since none exists. Instead, they address aspects of Anabaptist and Mennonite studies pertinent to the future of these churches. Precisely that future dimension compels CHS publication.

SERIES EDITOR'S FOREWORD

Searching for Sacred Ground, volume 7 in the C. Henry Smith Series, tells several stories. The most obvious story is that of Lawrence Hart, Cheyenne Peace Chief and ordained Mennonite minister. Chief Hart is a remarkable man—a presence that inspires commitment and courage and a desire to act justly. Only the heartless will remain unmoved by Hart's story.

A second explicit story is author Raylene Hinz-Penner's discovery of Lawrence Hart's story, from his May 1998 commencement address at Bethel College, the opening scene of the book, to her attendance at a Cheyenne Sun Dance, the account which shapes the book's culminating chapter. Hinz-Penner's personal involvement is important for this book. Beyond the standard data of his family genealogy, education and career path, through her eyes and ears the reader encounters the person of Lawrence Hart. It is through Hinz-Penner's questions and efforts to understand Cheyenne culture that readers experience a nonlinear world view, one different from a European, Western fixation on chronology, specific family genealogy, linear progression, and a fixed, centering view point. At times Hinz-Penner's expression of not understanding conveys that she really has entered a different world and world view. The answers to many questions during her visit to the Sun Dance "were often lost on me," she writes. "One must grow up with this ritual. The explanations were hollow; it is in the doing. It is in the being." Neither Raylene Hinz-Penner nor Lawrence Hart explains this worldview specifically—that would be already to subvert it—but aware readers can discover it.

Through the stories of Hinz-Penner and Hart, the reader will encounter other stories. The verses of the well-known national hymn,

"America the Beautiful," speak of America's good crowned with "broth-erhood," of the "pilgrim feet" that "a thoroughfare for freedom beat across the wilderness," of the heroes who loved "mercy more than life." Without making a point of it, the narratives of both Hinz-Penner and of Hart belie those words, which actually fit the native people, and most certainly Lawrence Hart, more than the song's claimed subjects.

Although *Searching for Sacred Ground* is not a theology book, it participates in the conversation about the relationship of Christianity to culture. The book will bring non-Native readers to awareness of how European and Western their religious practices are, and thereby will serve as a profound statement that it is possible to express the meaning of the Christian story through non-European cultures and traditions.

Chief Hart's story is one of participation in and interweaving of multiple stories—of the survival of the Cheyenne people in the face of white, European immigration, the intersection and interaction of Hart's Cheyenne people and Hinz-Penner's Mennonite people on the plains of Oklahoma. Hart often pictures the interaction via circles—an interaction is completed by a later kind of return. The Bethel commencement address with which Penner opens her narrative completes such a circle between Mennonites and Cheyennes.

I was once privileged to hear and participate in the completion of a such circle. In late August 2002, Lawrence Hart gave the address in the opening convocation at Bluffton University. Samuel K. Mosiman, the second president of Bluffton University, had served for six years as superintendent of the Mennonite Cheyenne-Arapahoe Indian Mission School at Cantonment, Oklahoma before acquiring more education and moving to then Central Mennonite College in 1908 and assuming the presidency a year later. As Hart told it, Mosiman's work in the school at Cantonment had been a Mennonite contribution to the native peoples. Now, a hundred years later, with Hart's journey to minister in Bluffton, a Cheyenne offering was being given to Mennonites in return—and a circle was completed. As an image of that completed circle, Hart asked to have a picture taken of himself with Mosiman Hall, the building on the Bluffton campus bearing the name of S. K. Mosiman. I felt like I was performing a sacred duty when I found a photographer to take the picture for Chief Hart.

Many thanks to Mennonite Historical Society, co-sponsor with Bluffton University of the Smith series, for generous support of this volume's publication. I am grateful to Raylene Hinz-Penner for this manuscript—grateful that she followed up the impulse to learn to know Chief Hart and to tell this story, and grateful that she entrusted the manuscript to the C. Henry Smith Series for publication. It has been a delight to work with her as an author. I have no doubt that readers will share my gratitude to Hinz-Penner for producing this marvelous manuscript.

Above all I am grateful to Chief Lawrence Hart for allowing Hinz-Penner to tell this story. He gave many hours of his time in interviews and in showing sites to Hinz-Penner. And beyond his time, Chief Hart gave his story—gave himself—to this project. I trust that readers will treasure this gift as much as I do.

—*J. Denny Weaver, Editor*
  The C. Henry Smith Series

AUTHOR'S PREFACE

Though I was born, raised, and schooled in the far western corner of Kansas just east of Liberal, I always knew that I was an Oklahoman. I was in Kansas by virtue of the fluke of my parents' purchase of land north of the border, the land they had found to buy while they lived in the little Mennonite community of Turpin in the Oklahoma Panhandle. Virtually no one else in our church farmed in Kansas. My parents had moved from Clinton in central Oklahoma a year before I was born—to Turpin where my father's oldest brother lived. Early in my parents' marriage in the late 1940s, they, like so many other post-war newlyweds, were seeking opportunity.

Our lives revolved around Friedensfeld, our little Turpin, Oklahoma Mennonite Church, and our extended family—twelve sets of uncles and aunts, grandparents, great-grandparents—all of whom lived in Oklahoma. I had always been especially interested in my central Oklahoma family and their lives along the Washita River on Oklahoma's red soil—as well as their Cheyenne and Arapaho neighbors. When our family returned there to visit and drove along Clinton's Main Street where both my parents had worked, they would point to old chiefs in their long braids wrapped in blankets and sitting on benches in the sun—and try to remember their names. They reviewed the names they knew from school or church—like Heap of Birds. I remember sitting in the back seat of our green Mercury and wondering how life might be different if one had a name with a literal referent like "heap of birds."

My father died young in the 1970s. I settled in central Kansas, where I taught college English at my alma mater, Bethel College. Years later, in the 1990s, I found myself going back to central Oklahoma to Corn for

15

funerals. My father's siblings were buried at the Bergthal Mennonite Church cemetery. I remember standing under the Oklahoma sky as Reverend Lawrence Hart from Clinton conducted my Aunt Ruth's burial service. The recitation of familiar Bible passages over my Aunt Ruth's open grave by the famous Cheyenne Peace Chief, Reverend Lawrence H. Hart, was a moment of recognition for me. These two peoples—the immigrant Mennonites and the relocated Cheyennes—had shared a life in Oklahoma. As a Mennonite minister, Reverend Hart felt like a part of the family. I went home and wrote the following poem after Aunt Ruth's burial. I see now that it was the beginning of this book. Chief Hart's commencement address a few years later at Bethel College actually launched my research.

Ceremony

This country's greatest living peace chief among the Cheyennes
is burying my Aunt Ruth in the hard red dirt of Bergthal
Cemetery north of Corn. We stand on ground my ancestors
gave beside old stones that bear the family name. One by one,
they bring us home. Last year my cousin came with her father
to bury his old kin and mounted the hill in procession to find
the dead man's beautiful horse, standing tall above an open grave.

Chief Hart gathers us round Aunt Ruth, his dark hand
pointed like an arrow at the sky. Over the wind which sweeps
round the now long-vacant church, his deep voice speaks:
The Lord giveth and the Lord taketh away;
blessed be the name of the Lord.
What we have left are words we have agreed to share.
We bring them back from half-remembered pasts to believe anew,
take them home from here to test against our lives—our history
now the crazy spinning of a thousand stories we love into earth's
silence, forgetfulness. We hang on tight to his words, erect them
with wonder in the open air—as if we could build a place
on a new frontier, as if we could walk inside it and worship.
(earlier version printed in *What Mennonites Are Thinking*, 1998)

I offer my sincere thanks to Lawrence and Betty Hart for giving me so many hours of their time, for letting me into their lives, for sharing their stories. I appreciated the helpful suggestions of C. Henry Smith series editor J. Denny Weaver and the reviewers who read this manuscript as well as the work of Michael A. King, publisher, Cascadia Publishing House. I wish to thank my mother and sister, who encouraged this work. My deepest thanks goes to my husband Doug who, as president of Bethel College, invited Hart to speak at commencement. Later, when I began this research, Doug listened, advised, traveled with me, and even read an early draft when I needed that. His support and encouragement have been invaluable.

LAWRENCE HART
BIOGRAPHICAL SKETCH

Dr. Bob Blackburn, Executive Director of the Oklahoma Historical Society, calls Lawrence Hart an "Oklahoma treasure." While interviewing Hart, I discovered that he is much more. Historically, he represents a unique bridge to the Cheyenne peace traditions of an earlier time. He is also a national treasure, a dynamic and creative force in this country for mediation, restoration, conciliation, and preservation.

Lawrence H. Hart, a principal traditional peace chief of the Cheyennes and an ordained Mennonite minister, grew up near Hammon, Oklahoma. Today he directs the Cheyenne Cultural Center east of Clinton, where he has lived for more than forty years. He has been a delegate to the White House Conference on Indian Education and Indian Elder of the Year as delegated by the National Indian Education Association. The Oklahoma Heritage Association awarded him the Distinguished Service Award. U.S. Secretary Bruce Babbitt appointed Hart to the Review Committee of the Native American Graves Protection and Repatriation Act of 1990 on which he served eight years. His service led to his successful repatriation of Cheyenne ancestors' remains and his ongoing efforts to repatriate more than 100,000 remaining unidentified native remains.

Hart testified at hearings in Congress that the site where his ancestors died along the Washita River at the hands of Custer's Seventh Cavalry was sacred ground, leading to the establishment of the Washita Battlefield National Historic Site operated by the National Park Service near Cheyenne, Oklahoma. He established the Cheyenne Heritage Trail Tour and the Cheyenne Cultural Center, where Cheyenne traditions, art, and language are preserved. As a Cheyenne peace chief, a living reminder of the Washita attack, at the televised memorial service he was asked to read the first forty-two names of the 168 victims in the Murrah Building bombing in Oklahoma City. He is an advisor on the Oklahoma judicial team developing an ongoing educational exhibit, "The Cheyenne Way of Justice," designed to teach a restorative justice model which predates current U.S. models of justice. The Oklahoma Supreme Court honored Chief Hart with the Friend of the Court Medal at the Sixteenth Annual Sovereignty Symposium in 2003.

Hart travels widely as a speaker, consultant, advisor, and committee member for his tribe, his church, and his country. He is married to Betty (Bartel) Hart, who manages the Cheyenne Cultural Center and ministers in the church. Lawrence and Betty have three children: Connie, married to Gordon Yellowman; Nathan, married to Melanie (Stucky); and Cristina. They have four grandchildren: Cristina Yellowman, Micah, Lily and Sydney Hart, and Lexus Wolfe.

PROLOGUE: *AXIS MUNDI*

*I*n my capacity as one of the peace chiefs, I have for the past few months
searched for a special cottonwood tree. Such a tree must be large enough to
have at least forty growth rings. It must be straight and tall and have a
fork, with both branches of the fork of equal size. When such a tree is
found, it will be selected and cut to be used as a center pole in an annual
"renewal of the earth" ceremony the Cheyenne people conduct on or near
the summer solstice the twenty-first of June. . . .
—Hart, "Connections" 1998, 1

This story begins with commencement.

    Peace Chief Lawrence H. Hart of the Southern Cheyennes was de-
livering the commencement address to the 105th graduating class of
Bethel College, a Mennonite school in North Newton, Kansas on May
24, 1998. He is a distinguished alumnus of the college and a minister of
the Mennonite denomination which founded and still supports it. He
came on this day to tell his audience a story, a story of his own Cheyenne
traditions and history and to explain how that story is interwoven with
the story of the Mennonites who came to the plains states in the 1870s.
And underneath that history lesson is his own belief in a destiny, a divine
design which has placed him on the Memorial Hall stage before us.

> In addition to looking for that special tree, I am also searching for
> the site of such a renewal of the earth ceremony that took place in
> summer 1868. That year all of our people should have been on a
> reservation in what is now Oklahoma, subsequent to the Medi-
> cine Lodge Treaty of 1867. It turns out not all of our people were
> on a reservation for somewhere along Walnut Creek in west cen-

tral Kansas, a group of our people conducted that very same renewal of the earth ceremony. There are two forks of the Walnut
Creek northwest of Fort Larned and if the land has not been dis-
turbed, such as by plowing, the location of the ceremonial lodge
will be evident. To locate the site will be an awesome experience.
Right in the middle of that circle, evidenced by contrasting vegetation, will be where a center pole stood. The center pole, of the
same kind of cottonwood I am helping to look for, served as the
axis mundi, a symbolic center of the earth. The axis mundi is a
point between heaven and earth and is viewed as the most sacred
spot in this meaningful ceremony that renews the earth. (Hart,
"Connections" 1998, 1-2)

I have since learned that the Renewal of the Earth or the Cheyenne
Medicine Lodge ceremony (the Sun Dance) is, in fact, a reenactment of
the creation of the world. Though I was unaware of the ceremony's sacred significance when Chief Hart described it that day, in that moment
as I sat in Hart's audience in Memorial Hall, I grasped that he was con-
necting our peoples through history in a way that I had not previously
understood. He was beginning to recreate a world of interlinking des-
tinies that had existed between the Cheyenne people and the Mennonites on the Central Plains.

Hart's commencement address that May afternoon wound itself
deeper and deeper into history. He connected his own Cheyenne tribal
roots to Siberia, citing Douglas Comer's *Ritual Ground*. In this work the
ritual acts of the Cheyenne Renewal of the Earth ceremony are related to
those of Siberian groups who also used a center pole—a birch tree rather
than a cottonwood—as an *axis mundi*. Hart posited the migration trek
of his people from Siberia to this hemisphere over Beria, ice which once
covered the Bering Strait, then down through Alaska, the Northwest
Territories, to the Great Lakes area where they were living by the time of
Columbus' arrival on this continent. He traced the Cheyenne place
names left by their migration through the Dakotas, Wyoming, Nebraska, Colorado, Kansas, and finally, to the reservation in Oklahoma in
the area where his grandparents, parents, and he himself grew up near
Hammon, Oklahoma.

Then Chief Hart did what I would later learn he always does: he en-
larged the tribe. He brought the Mennonites into the tent! He spoke of
the significant migrations of Mennonites from Russia to Kansas in the

years following those when the Cheyennes were placed on an Oklahoma reservation. Shortly after their arrival in Kansas, these same Mennonites built Bethel College, the oldest Mennonite college in the United States, and Chief Hart's alma mater. At the same time, U.S. President Ulysses Grant, at the urging of the Quakers, who with many others in this country were outraged by the violence and injustice which had been perpetrated upon the Native peoples on the plains, adopted a "peace policy." That policy included assigning the Quakers as Indian agents to help educate the newly located Cheyenne and Arapaho tribes. These Quakers contacted their fellow pacifists, newly arrived Mennonites in Kansas, to come help serve as teachers and staff in their new educational venture at Darlington School, named for the first Quaker agent, Brinton Darlington.

> The Mennonites came. Young Cheyenne students were there. Two distinct peoples, with two vastly different histories, very far apart in terms of their culture, now began to develop connections with each other. Education was central in this first connection between these two peoples of vastly different histories and cultures. (Hart, "Connections" 1998, 6-7)

Chief Hart described how, when Bethel College decision-makers looked to find a president for its new institution, they tapped Cornelius H. Wedel and his wife, Susie Richert, both of whom had worked at the Darlington School on the Cheyenne and Arapaho Reservation; Wedel would serve as president for seventeen years. And as he spoke, Hart offered himself as the embodiment of the two peoples' history on the Plains:

> On this day as the 105th graduating class of Bethel College holds their commencement, I have the distinct honor to be invited to come from our former reservation area to deliver the commencement address. I am awed. This is an axis mundi. (Hart, "Connections" 1998, 7-8)

My memory of the moment in which Hart made his pronouncement was that I could not breathe. From the point in his address at which Hart had said that he hoped he might find the 1868 spot on Walnut Creek unplowed, I had become keenly aware of two peoples, the Cheyennes and the Mennonites, together on these Plains, and now gathered together in the person of Lawrence Hart. Mennonites came to Kansas to farm; they had plowed the sacred sites. My grandparents migrated in 1874 from that area in Russia to which he broadly connects his own ancient Siberian roots. They came first to Kansas and then journeyed to Oklahoma, where all of my people bought and farmed land formerly granted to the Cheyenne and Arapaho tribes among Cheyenne and Arapaho allotments.

> Centuries ago, the Cheyenne were in Siberia. Just over a century ago, some Mennonites were in the country of Russia at the invitation of Catherine the Great. Circumstances necessitated a migration from the Steppes of Russia to this country. Would the Cheyenne and the Mennonites, peoples so vastly different from each other, ever have a connection? (Hart, "Connections" 1998, 6)

I was learning that indeed, the two peoples had been connected now for well over a century, and emblematic of that center pole that reached between heaven and earth, serving some destiny, as he himself seemed to see it, stood Mennonite minister and Cheyenne Peace Chief Hart himself.

I would learn in the years that followed his address that day that Hart is in the business of constructing and restoring sacred sites. I would learn that he has spent a lifetime searching for renewable sites on the earth. Proclaiming the Memorial Hall stage where he stood that day "a point at which heaven and earth meet"—where the earth so often desecrated by our own lives might be renewed in some sense—pulled at something deep within me and would not let me go. I had to find out more about the connections between these two peoples. Eventually, my interest in seeking out that story led me directly to Chief Hart himself in Oklahoma.

Searching for
Sacred Ground

ONE
CHAPTER

SOUTH TO OKLAHOMA

The granddaddy I never knew was a truck driver on these Oklahoma highways I drive today, as was my daddy at age seventeen after my granddaddy's early death. It must be their blood in my veins that makes me love to drive. I sometimes wonder if this is some deep longing of plains peoples, on horseback or by vehicle, to cover the land? When the roadside sign says, "Tucumcari Tonight, Heart of Route 66"—for a moment, I decide to go! On my car's radio Garrison Keillor is reading from Walt Whitman's "Song of Myself":

A child said What is the grass? Fetching it to me with full hands,
How could I answer the child? . . .
I guess it is the handkerchief of the Lord,
A scented gift and remembrancer designedly dropt, . . .
And now it seems to me the beautiful uncut hair of graves. . . .
I pass death with the dying and birth with the new-wash'd babe,
    and am not contain'd between my hat and boots, . . .

That is what driving does for me, I think, especially in Oklahoma; I always feel that I am passing the "beautiful uncut hair of graves" I should discover and know. Like Whitman, while driving one feels oneself not necessarily contained between one's hat and boots.

I began the drive south this November morning in the dark, a long morning's drive from my home in central Kansas to Custer County, where Peace Chief Lawrence Hart will be awaiting our first appointed interview at the Cheyenne Cultural Center. I love motoring south over the land, watching for the first sign that the soil has gone red. I anticipate again the change of terrain that happens when one enters the miles of Oklahoma pastureland, open vistas, buttes, rivers, and canyons.

My people are all Oklahomans; all of them lived in Washita and Custer counties since the early days of settlement. Rural people, they always identified with the land—the sections and quarter sections they farmed, the land someone inherited, the land someone lost in the Depression, the Washita River they played in, the neighbors west or south.

And my family stories included references to their Cheyenne and Arapaho neighbors. When my mother was a girl in the 1930s, and her parents farmed just outside Corn in Washita County, their landlords, the White Turtles, paid long summer visits to the land my grandparents leased from them.

Nearing the Oklahoma border, it grows light.

The place names I begin to record pique my imagination: Do I know a story about Black Bear Creek? Was Anadarko where my father's brakes went out when he was hauling a heavy truckload in the '40s?

By seven o'clock, the southeast horizon glows: heavy pink has slid itself solidly under the cloud bank. The billboard says, "Cowboy Trailer Sales." I am in Oklahoma. I note the herd of longhorn cattle. Braum's Ice Cream . . . Guthrie, the old territorial capital.

"Where the West Begins. . . ."

Oklahoma running horses are advertised, and ahead a fresh load of bright green alfalfa bales on a gooseneck trailer is pulled easily by the standard white pickup all of my Oklahoma uncles drive—their license tags embossed with the Indian shield.

And now, I am coming out of the fog into Oklahoma county:

Oklahoma City, where Lawrence Hart, Peace Chief, was selected as one of the people delegated to read on national television the names of those killed in the bombing of the Murrah Federal Building at the first memorial service. Oklahoma City . . . what does it mean to Hart? My Oklahoma kin have referred to it all the years of my life as simply "The City"—as in answer to the question, "Where is Uncle Elmer?"

"They took him to The City to his heart doctor."

Driving west through Yukon, by the North Canadian River toward El Reno and Chickasha, I cross the Chisholm Trail at El Reno.

"Hitchhikers may be escaping inmates." I am fifty-seven miles from Clinton and the Cheyenne Cultural Center. Cherokee Buffalo Burgers.

Low red sumac. And then, Roman Nose State Park, where we gather for family reunions.

But I cannot remember who Roman Nose was. An outlaw? A Cheyenne chief? Geary, Watonga, Caddo County. The names reflect the many tribes who ended up in Oklahoma—big tourist business now as Oklahoma too emphasizes heritage. Hinton, Anadarko, Red Rock Canyon State Park.

The Wichita Mountains are visible in the distance. Finally I am in Custer County. All of those visitors to my childhood home in southwest Kansas with Custer County vehicle license tags, and I never thought of the blonde-haired general. For me, Custer was a place.

One can make a car trip following the path General Custer took to get to the Washita battle site near Cheyenne. Chief Lawrence Hart has marked with road signs this Cheyenne Heritage Trail, beginning in Kansas with the beautifully preserved Fort Larned. The fort is one of those military headquarters caught in the strange paradox of purposes known to the early settlement era: The fort housed those required to seek out and destroy the Cheyenne people where they "impeded progress"—but it also served them as a safe haven, source of food, and protection, usually housing the Indian agent to the tribe. This trail goes through Fort Supply, near Woodward, Oklahoma, where we went to the rodeo every fall as I was growing up, and on to the Washita battle site.

A couple of years ago, with a group of college students, I followed the path of General Custer's wintry journey in 1868 to track down the Cheyennes, the journey that culminated in the fateful attack by Custer's troops on Hart's tribal ancestor, Peace Chief Black Kettle and his camp. Chief Black Kettle and his wife Medicine Woman Later lost their lives in the icy waters of the Washita that fateful day, and the tribe lost its autonomy. Today, that Washita Battlefield near Cheyenne is a National Historic Site being restored to its 1868 state as a place to tell this story, thanks in part to the work of Cheyenne Peace Chief Hart.

Chief Hart's silver pickup, a Nissan Road Runner, is parked outside the Cheyenne Cultural Center on Route 66 on the outer edge of Clinton near the Washita River. I make my way along the sidewalk beside the now dry but carefully marked herbs and plants traditionally used by the Cheyennes: sumac, coralberry, slender greenthread for Indian tea, yarrow, coneflower, sweet grass for incense in ceremonies, sand plum, gooseberry, and more. They have cultivated some twenty-five varieties

of plants used by the Cheyennes for medicinal purposes, food, and ceremony along the sidewalk which leads into the entry.

Hart is working on a paper, "The Legacy of Moving Behind," the
story of a young Cheyenne woman who survived the Washita attack. He
will deliver the keynote address for the Third Annual Cheyenne Symposium on the Battle of the Washita.

I note how handsome Chief Hart is. Not yet seventy, he carries himself with solemn dignity, in well-appointed clothing—a monogrammed
shirt, a fine cut of slacks. His decorum suggests respect for the interviewer, respect for the world, respect for those who would come to seek
him out at the Cheyenne Cultural Center. It is warm inside, the fans
blowing. Frankly, I am nervous to approach this man I so respect, fearful
of my own prodding, knowing I will unwittingly transgress on cultural
taboos. I know that Chief Hart's life and the time he shares with me are
gifts. Known for his generosity, he is constantly traveling on behalf of his
people, Cheyenne and Mennonite. The time I take will necessarily steal
him from work that matters to us all, and he needs more years to finish
his commitments than he will have.

My visit has been preceded only by a telephone request for an interview. Now, I try to tell Chief Hart what I have in mind, interviews to discover his personal story as a bridge to older times and ways—a recon-
struction of what happened between then and now, using his own life
story as center point. What can he tell me about how he got from the
Washita site I have visited to the stage of Memorial Hall where he stood
awestruck by this destiny? I tell him that he could write this himself, of
course, but I fear that he will not. Honestly, I do not know what to ask
for, so I simply ask again for some of his time to record some interviews.
I have brought a series of questions. If he will point me to key sites on
this journey, I will do the research to fill in the navigations from site to
site. He agrees to try to answer my questions.

When we are ready to record his responses, I have one last question:
what should I be careful of as we talk? Are there cultural taboos I will
transgress? I am anxious about posing even the first question. Chief Hart
is deliberate, as he always is; he wants to give an answer with integrity but
also to give me permission to go forward. He did not ask that anyone
trace his life's journey or try to ferret out his influences. I initiated all.
There is a long pause after my question, then he cautions quietly, "I
would not wish to be seen as boasting" (Hart, Interview Nov. 12, 2002).

CHAPTER TWO

TSIS-TSIS-TAS AND *SUTAIO*

We are part of the Red Moon band who settled around the Hammon area where we would eventually take our allotments. We are Sutaio. The story goes that there was a standoff long, long ago between the Cheyenne tribe and another tribe. And then, somehow, they recognized that they could understand one another's language, as they spoke understandable dialects of an Algonquian language. So, the two groups merged, began to live together. . . . My people are from that Sutaio group which merged with the Cheyennes. Therefore, I inherit the sometimes distinctive Sutaio cultural ways and beliefs. . . . I know that when the Mennonite missionary J. B. Ediger came to bring the good news to our tribe, the people wanted to give him a name, so they named him Sutaio after that distinct tribal group among the Cheyennes which they represented.
—Hart, Interview Nov. 12, 2002

Chief Hart's tribal ancestor, Chief Black Kettle, is usually considered the most famous and significant of the Cheyenne peace chiefs. Black Kettle, who had attempted to negotiate the Cheyennes through their hardest years until his death in 1868, was *Sutaio*, Chief Hart explained during our first interview. The Sutaio branch of the Cheyennes had linked up with the tribe (and substantially increased their numbers) during their stay along the Missouri River sometime during the years 1750-1780 (Berthrong, *The Southern Cheyennes* 1963, 10-11).

Even earlier, the Cheyennes, an Algonquian-speaking people who called themselves *Tsis-tsis-tas*—"we belong here" or "people" (Berthrong, *The Southern Cheyennes* 1963, 27), had lived an agricultural existence in earthen lodges for a half-century on the Sheyenne River of North Dakota (6). The name *Cheyenne*, as the tribe has come to be known, is actually an English corruption of the Sioux term *Shahi'ela* or *Shahi'ena* for "red speech" or speaking a foreign tongue (Chalfant, *Cheyennes and Horse Soldiers* 1989, 300). In the Cheyenne Heritage Trail brochure, the Cheyenne name is said to be taken from Sioux words meaning "people of alien speech"—referring to the Cheyenne's native Algonquian language. Cheyenne words for the tribe mean "people who are alike." The word *Cheyenne* is indicated by drawing the right index finger across the left several times. This means "striped arrows" and alludes to the tribe's preference for turkey feathers to wing their arrows.

While in the northern country, the Cheyennes acquired the horse and broadened their trading relationships, two events which would define their subsequent lifestyle and territories of habitation. They became dependent on buffalo to supplement their diet of beans, corn, and squash (Berthrong, *Southern Cheyennes* 1963, 6). They also had to become mobile because of their dependence on the horse and its needs for water and grass. Some Cheyennes must have lived at the same time along the Missouri River, where their economy was mixed, trading agricultural products along with their pursuit of buffalo (9).

The Sutaio who joined the Cheyennes reportedly still maintained separate camps, their own traditions, organization, lore, and culture heroes as late as the 1830s, eighty to 100 years after their groups had merged (Berthrong, *Southern Cheyennes* 1963, 27). Thus Chief Hart notes carefully, when he begins to tell me who he is, that Black Kettle and his band were *Sutaio*, buffalo people with the distinctive traditions Chief Hart himself inherited.

Early Cheyenne historian George Bird Grinnell notes that the amalgamation of the two tribes gave them two culture-heroes and two sacred objects: the medicine arrows brought by Sweet Medicine and the buffalo cap brought by *Suhtai* hero Straight Horns or Standing on the Ground (1907, 169). Each of these mythic heroes brought his own sacred stories, many about fending off starvation for the people.

The Cheyenne migrations west and south of the Missouri River were influenced by conflicts, especially with the Teton Sioux; by their desire for trade; and by their alignment with the Arapaho tribe, who first headed into the Black Hills (Berthrong, *Southern Cheyennes* 1963, 18-19). The Cheyennes were later found on the Arkansas River primarily because of their desire for wild horses. The Hairy Rope band, whose leadership includes Afraid of Beavers (Hart's great-grandfather), renowned for their ability to catch wild horses, were the first group of Cheyennes to move south, as far as the Cimarron River Valley (21). By 1821, when Jacob Fowler recorded in his journal his encounter with Cheyennes on his trek en route from Fort Smith to the Rocky Mountains, he found 200 lodges of Cheyennes along the Arkansas River (reported in Berthrong, 1963, 21). By the time Bent's Fort, a trading rather than a military post, was constructed in southeastern Colorado, the Cheyenne people centered their activities around this area and were able to conduct their trading much farther south of the Missouri River. By the 1830s their residences and trade had been removed south to sites along the Platte and Arkansas Rivers (Berthrong, 1963, 26).

Cheyenne life during the Plains settlement era has received a variety of interpretations. Elliott West used the Cheyenne tribe as a case study to show how they were drawn into the Plains drama by their own choices and two powerful inducements. First, the bison and the horse lured them away from village life, which they traded for nomadic life; and second, commerce drew them into special relationships with others settling the Plains. West believes the Cheyennes chose to play the role of "middle man" in the economic balance on the Plains. After they became dependent on the horse to carry out trade and a new way of life, they needed six horses for every man, woman, and child—and for security, up to twelve horses per person. The horse had become not only a necessity of the hunting life but also enhanced the Cheyenne warrior's prowess and mobility; became a means of exchange for negotiation and trade; and ultimately became the symbol of identity, status, and wealth.

West argued that the Cheyenne tribe's dependence on the buffalo upset the old tribal norms of work and power. When they had lived in the north on the Missouri River, Cheyenne women had controlled both the garden and the market; they had economic, social, and spiritual authority (West, 1998, 78). In the new warrior society, women became processors, comparable to factory workers, responsible for "the backbreaking labor of skinning bison and scraping, rubbing, and kneading the hides into pliable, saleable robes" (78). The histories document repeatedly how difficult life became for Cheyenne women in their attempt to survive the Plains economy.

Additionally, to secure power with the new white population flooding the Plains, the Cheyennes married their women to the traders. West noted, for example, that White Thunder, Keeper of the Sacred Arrows given the tribe by their prophet Sweet Medicine, married his daughter to William Bent, builder of Bent's Fort. Indeed, this marriage followed in the traditional pattern practiced by Plains tribes, an old pattern designed for keeping the peace among warring tribes. However, West believes that the subsequent reliance of the Cheyennes on Bent's Fort pulled them south and away from their spiritual base, Bear Butte (Cheyenne "Noaha-vose"). Atop Bear Butte, Sweet Medicine received the Sacred Arrows which he gave to the Cheyennes with the promise that as long as the arrows were kept, the Cheyenne people would continue to exist. This event in their mythology is comparable to Moses receiving the Ten Commandments in the Old Testament.

Because not all the Cheyennes agreed to rebase operations at Bent's Fort, those who remained along the North Platte eventually became the Northern Cheyennes. Those who moved to a home range along the Arkansas became Southern Cheyennes. In addition, their groups had to be smaller and smaller because of the increased dependence on horses, perhaps eventually at a ratio of 400 horses for forty people. To provide range area for the horses, the tribe had to spread itself thin: "November to April, Plains peoples had no choice but to break up into small groups" (West, 1998, 84). By placing themselves squarely into the middle of the Plains ferment as economic "middle men," West contends that the Cheyenne systems of government, spirituality, cultural roles, lifestyle, were all pulled apart, splintered in irreparable ways.

Some time after I had completed early interviews with Chief Hart, I had occasion to visit Bent's Fort in Colorado near LaJunta. I was enroute to the Four Corners area, retracing a journey Chief Hart had often made as a child with his grandfather, John P. Hart, to visit the Ute Mountain Ute Reservation. Bent's Fort was a hub for Cheyenne activity as white traders and Plains settlers began to cross the Central Plains. Here, the Cheyennes, most prominent of the players in the Bent's Fort saga of Plains settlement, used that theater of interaction among the Europeans, the Spanish/Mexicans, and themselves to maintain important rituals of civility, to balance relations, and maintain their autonomy. Eventually, the loss of that world of ritual centered around trade relations at Bent's Fort would lead to the atrocities of Sand Creek committed against the Cheyennes—and four years later on the Washita River against Black Kettle and his tribe, Chief Hart's ancestors.

> The cessation of ritualized relations with Native Americans culminated in a campaign of extermination, typified by the horrendous massacre at Sand Creek where men, women and children were killed and mutilated in ritualistic ways that denied their human status.
>
> The symbolism of this atrocity was to have a profoundly destructive effect on Native American-Anglo-American relations. The Cheyenne and Arapaho became implacable foes of the Anglos, and they were ultimately removed from the vicinity of Bent's Old Fort to reservations in Oklahoma. (West, 1998, 31)

When I visited the restored contemporary Bent's Fort near LaJunta, I went looking for signs of the Cheyenne sojourn there. Of course, one saw the obvious: the buffalo hide press in the very center of the fort, which squeezed ten robes into a tight bundle for efficient shipping of thousands of the hides. One could purchase a well-known sketch of dancing Cheyenne women. The reconstructed trading store shows the wares offered the tribes—cloth, beads, butcher knives, guns, powder, kettles, and blankets, one of which might be worth ten buffalo robes! Our tour guide took us to the top of the wall to point out where the Cheyenne and Arapaho tribes camped near the Fort along the river.

However, I could not understand until I had studied Comer's *Ritual Ground* (1996), first recommended by Chief Hart himself during his commencement address, that the 1833 meteor shower which the Cheyennes had interpreted as a sign of the end of the world—their warriors sang their death songs—was, indeed, just that. As forces converged round the Cheyenne/Arapaho tribes who had thrown their lot in with this new trade enterprise at the very vortex of the "new world" created on the Plains, they would suffer most when the experiment exploded.

For a brief period Bent's Fort, that "Castle on the Plains"—the most remarkable structure at the time from the Mississippi to the Pacific— represented a kind of paradise. Bent's Fort was the host for ritual interaction among several peoples new to the Plains trying to find their way to new existence. But the Cheyennes were right to interpret the 1833 meteor shower as a forecast of the end of their world.

Meanwhile, for a quarter century the proprietors of Bent's Fort controlled the region from their fort. Clearly, the Cheyenne and Arapaho tribes held the highest status, being the only tribes among the native peoples to be sometimes allowed into the Fort (Comer, 1996, 90). Comer believes the intense desire for trade evidenced by the Cheyenne/Arapaho peoples was actually a "desire for enduring, kin-type relationship established by the ritual of trade much more than desire for the objects that might be obtained by trade" (110). In other words, trade was a ceremony which secured not just profit but a long-term practicality. The Cheyenne and Arapaho people understood their trading relationship as networking against a rainy day! But the Cheyennes had misjudged their partners. What they believed they secured through ritual trade was never real:

> A good example of such an imaginary relationship is that which the Native Americans believed to be symbolized by the peace medals, beads, firearms, and other trade objects presented to them by the whites. The Native Americans assumed that such items established a relationship of long-term reciprocal commitments, one essentially alien in the modern world. (Comer, 1996, 132)

Tobacco, alcohol, firearms—all highly desired by the Native tribes—were not so much wanted for their function, says Comer, as for their ritual significance. Firearms, for example, were not as functional for the Native warriors as their bows and arrows, but they were prized for status, for perceived kinship relations, for their "medicine." They represented ritual relations. And thus, for the Cheyennes, the medicine received via trade "secured a position in a world that was changing too rapidly and unpredictably for comfort, a world that threatened to spin out of control" (Comer, 1996, 157). So it was that "when the Cheyennes camped at Sand Creek the night before the massacre there by Chivington's cavalry, they raised the American flag, sure as they did this that it would keep them from harm" (Comer, 1996, 159).

Sand Creek, the 1864 massacre of Cheyennes, including several of their greatest chiefs, marked the end of the recognition of common humanity between the new Americans and the Cheyenne tribe. It occurred, at least in part, because they no longer had a space for ritual exchange and recognition of the other's traditions; thereafter, they demonized each other and acted accordingly.

Henceforth, the Cheyenne people were engaged in hostilities with the Plains settlers which would result in two terrible attacks. Both involved the peace chief Black Kettle and his wife, Medicine Woman Later—first at Sand Creek in what is known today as Colorado, then on the Washita site in current-day western Oklahoma—attacks only four years apart, almost to the day.

CHAPTER THREE

THE WASHITA

Chief Hart prayed in Cheyenne before we opened the gate to enter the site, before he told the story again, the story of that terrible day on the Washita in 1868 when Chief Black Kettle and his wife Medicine Woman Later died in the icy waters of the Washita. Black Kettle's horse was tied nearby his lodge when the attack by Custer's forces came at dawn, and he, with his wife mounted in front of him, fled by horseback into the river in search of an escape. Chief Hart envisioned the scene for a group of college students: both Black Kettle and his wife were shot when they had almost crossed the Washita, both falling down into its cold waters. "I have often imagined their deaths that November morning in the icy Washita. I see them diving or hurled from their horse into the frozen waters. Last night as I was falling asleep, I thought about their martyrdom, its similarity to some of the Anabaptist martyr stories you would know from The Martyr's Mirror. . . . Felix Mantz, for example, the Anabaptist martyr in Zurich, was bound and drowned in the cold January waters of the Limmat River."

Chief Hart has spent a good portion of his adult life exploring Black Kettle's story, recounting that story, indeed preserving the great peace chief's memory and legacy through the establishment of a national historic site on the Washita where Black Kettle died near Cheyenne, Oklahoma.

Each time I have accompanied Chief Hart over the site which holds the blood of his ancestors, before he enters the site itself he prays in

Cheyenne in a strong deep voice that echoes out into the open sky. The prayer is in Cheyenne and I do not understand its words. I do understand that it is in recognition of the hallowed ground we will walk on where his ancestors lost their lives. What does he pray for? Forgiveness for all of us? A blessing on the memory? Gratitude for the Cheyenne tradition of peace for which Black Kettle was martyred? Those of us who have walked the site with Chief Hart recognize his deep reverence for this ancestral site, his pain as he recounts what happened there that day from the moment of Custer's surprise attack at dawn on his people to the soldiers' final act of killing the tribe's 800 ponies and their subsequent groans and death cries which lasted for hours where they lay shot.

My first trip to the Washita Battle Site was at dawn, the time of the attack. As we arrived, there was silence except for the coyotes howling nearby in the hills. In that hush we began walking the site and reliving the story. I knew, as I walked that site with Chief Hart, that his own life in Oklahoma actually begins here. After Black Kettle, there is direct descent to Chief Hart's own ancestors, descendants who witnessed the massacre. After Black Kettle, the Cheyennes were confined to Oklahoma, their days of freely roaming the Plains at an end. After Black Kettle begins Chief Hart's story. Those who raised Hart knew those who knew Chief Black Kettle.

In 1840 the Cheyenne and Arapaho tribes had made peace with the Comanches and Kiowas at Bent's Fort. In so doing, they had won the right to range south of the Arkansas River. The Treaty of Fort Laramie, the second Cheyenne treaty with the U.S. Government, was negotiated in 1851 by chiefs who preceded Black Kettle as principals. Chief Black Kettle may have first appeared as a principal peace chief with White Antelope, Tall Bear, and Lean Bear at Bent's place in 1857 (Hoig, *Peace Chiefs*, 1980, 106). At any rate, by 1860 he was firmly in place as principal chief of the Cheyennes for a treaty council: "From then until his death [in 1868] Black Kettle was clearly, as Cheyenne squawman John Prowers put it, *the* principal man of the tribe, even when in disfavor with the warring element" (106).

What one sees when one reads the various accounts of Black Kettle's turbulent years of leadership from 1860 to 1868 is his absolute, unflagging desire to make peace with the whites, even when his own people were totally disenchanted. This stubborn maintenance of the peace position on the part of Black Kettle is not sheer naivete or treason to a tribe's needs. His own Dog Soldiers must have interpreted it as "caving in to power" when he signed the various treaties which so angered the warriors. However, Black Kettle was simply keeping the vows the peace chief takes when he agrees to take on this leadership role.

Chief Hart has frequently recounted for audiences the ceremonies which occur when a new chief is "taken in" or installed as a peace chief. Before the giving of gifts, the sealing of the deal, the new chief must be made to understand what he is undertaking, what he has agreed to. To that end, the new chief is given as instruction the words of Sweet Medicine, the tribal hero who appointed the first Cheyenne chiefs.

> You chiefs are peacemakers. Though your son might be killed in front of your tepee, you should take a peace pipe and smoke. Then you would be called an honest chief. You chiefs own the land and the people. If your men, your soldier societies, should be scared and retreat, you are not to step back but take a stand to protect your land and your people. Get out and talk to the people. If strangers come, you are the ones to give presents to them and invitations. When you meet someone, or he comes to your tepee asking for anything, give it to him. Never refuse. Go outside your tepee and sing your chief's song, so all the people will know you have done something good. (quoted in Hoig, *Peace Chiefs* 1963, 7)

This is the vow Lawrence Hart himself has taken, the choice he has made for how he must live his life.

Interpreting Sweet Medicine's mandate, a peace chief is expected "to be a man of peace, to be brave, and to be of generous heart. Of these qualities the first was unconditionally the most important, for upon it rested the restraint required for the warlike Cheyenne nation" (Hoig, *Peace Chiefs* 1963, 7-8). Indeed, Chief Black Kettle would eventually become estranged from his own people by trying to keep this first and most significant of the vows.

One sees best Chief Black Kettle's peacemaking efforts and character in the events just preceding Sand Creek. Numerous conflicts had erupted between Cheyenne warriors and white settlers on the central Plains during that summer of 1864. Black Kettle tried to intervene, sending a letter to Fort Lyon offering to make peace and exchange prisoners. Major Wynkoop, in charge of Fort Lyon, came out to meet Chief Black Kettle on the Smoky Hill River, bringing with him his whole garrison force, which only further agitated the volatile Cheyenne Dog Soldiers. Furthermore, Wynkoop refused to deal. Chief Black Kettle apparently saw immediately that he must pour oil over the troubled waters: he embraced Wynkoop before his soldiers, took his hand, and offered publicly not just words of trust in Major Wynkoop but an understanding of Wynkoop's need to get clearance from the

> Great Father in Washington who must tell his soldiers to bury the hatchet, before we can again roam over the Prairies in safety and hunt the buffalo. Had this white soldier come to us with crooked words, I myself would have despised him; and would have asked whether he thought we were fools, that he could sing sweet words into our ears, and laugh at us when we believed them. But he has come with words of truth; and confidence, in the pledges of his Red brothers, and whatever be the result of these deliberations, he shall return unharmed to his lodge from whence he came. It is I Moka-ta-va-tah that says it. (quoted in Hoig, *Peace Chiefs* 1963, 109)

This is the enduring legacy of Chief Black Kettle—this willingness to stake his good name and his role as principal chief on negotiating, showing good faith even when he could no longer control his own people and long after they had lost faith in him.

Following the meeting with Major Wynkoop, Chief Black Kettle used his own ponies in trade to secure the release of captives and deliver them to Wynkoop. After this the chiefs Black Kettle, White Antelope, and Bull Bear, along with four Arapaho chiefs, went to Denver for a council with Governor Evans. Here, on September 28, 1864, two months to the day before the Sand Creek Massacre, Chief Black Kettle made an ardent plea on behalf of his people for peace:

> All we ask is that we may have peace with the whites; we want to hold you by the hand. You are our father; we have been traveling through a cloud; the sky has been dark ever since the war began. These braves who are with me are all willing to do what I say. We want to take good tidings home to our people, that they may sleep in peace. I want you to give all the chiefs of the soldiers here to understand that we are for peace. And that we have made peace, that we may not be mistaken by them for enemies. I have not come here with a little wolf's bark, but have come to talk

plain with you. We must live near the buffalo or starve. When we came here we came free, without any apprehension, to see you, and when I go home and tell my people that I have taken your hand and the hands of all the chiefs here in Denver, they will feel well, and so will all the different tribes of Indians on the Plains, after we have eaten and drunk with them. (quoted in Hoig, *Peace Chiefs* 1963, 110)

Seemingly, as evidenced by Chief Black Kettle's words here, he continued to believe that he could deliver peace as well and to retain confidence in the good-faith bargaining process. However, the peacemaker chief's pleas went unheeded. Wynkoop was replaced by Major Scott Anthony, who instructed Black Kettle to keep his people on Sand Creek. There they were attacked on November 28, 1864, by Colonel Chivington, "willingly supported by Major Anthony" (Hoig, *Peace Chiefs* 1963, 111).

When Chief Black Kettle was alerted that troops were coming toward his camp on Sand Creek, he went into his lodge and got a large American flag given to him earlier. White Antelope helped him tie the flag to a lodge pole along with a white flag, and he stood waving it in front of his tipi. The troops fired, surrounding the village. Black Kettle remained there as women and children fled. Finally, he took his wife to follow the others up the creek. When she was shot and appeared to be dead, Black Kettle struggled on without her, and she was shot eight more times, but survived. Black Kettle returned for her when the soldiers finally withdrew.

More than one hundred Cheyennes were killed, the camp destroyed, hundreds of horses and mules captured, and several Cheyenne chiefs slaughtered. Of course, the Cheyenne warriors retaliated. "The Dog Soldiers, indifferent to the fact that it had been Colorado whites who massacred the Cheyenne village, ripped up the lines of transportation and frontier settlements throughout Kansas" (Hoig, *Peace Chiefs* 1963, 112).

Black Kettle now lost control, completely disgraced. But he kept trying, while acknowledging that he could not be held responsible for the acts of some of his soldiers. Along with others he signed a new treaty at Medicine Lodge in 1867 to move to a reserve area in the northern part of what was called Indian Territory. He continued to defend the Cheyennes against charges brought against them, and he bargained in good faith with the whites again and again despite the open threats of his own Dog Soldiers, who at least on one occasion even corralled him to keep him from going forward to meet again for peace talks (Hoig, *Peace Chiefs* 1963, 115).

In his "Prologue" to *Cheyennes at Dark Water Creek*, William Chalfant recounts the treaty disasters for the Cheyennes. He argues that Cheyenne governing structures were simply not designed to make treaties work. Using the Treaty of the Little Arkansas in 1865 as his example, he contends,

> For the whites, the treaties salved their consciences and provided a legal instrument on which to base a claim of title. No matter that only four chiefs of the Council of Forty-Four (the only legitimate forum for decisions relating to the entire Cheyenne tribe) signed the Treaty of the Little Arkansas, or even knew of it until months had passed. No matter that the treaty named Black Kettle—one of four council chiefs of the Wutapui band and a strong advocate of peace as the only means of survival—as head-chief of all the Cheyenne tribe (which he was not), and provided that his word would bind all members of the tribe (which it could not). In fact, no Cheyenne chief had the authority to bind other tribal members—something few whites ever understood. (1998, xvi)

Chief Black Kettle was much involved and implicated in the treaty talks at Medicine Lodge which would again relocate the Cheyenne reserve area. Clearly, at Medicine Lodge, "the Cheyennes, at best, presented but a disjointed front" (Greene 2004, 106). Cheyenne soldiers were involved in more atrocities along the Saline and Solomon rivers.

Eventually, then, Black Kettle had only fifty lodges on the Washita, and as late as November 20, 1868, just days before Custer descended on his little village on the Washita, he met with General Hazen at Fort Cobb. General Hazen admitted in that meeting with Black Kettle that Sheridan was even then out fighting the Indians, and that Black Kettle would need to go back 100 miles to his camp and try to make his own peace with Sheridan.

Upon his return to camp along the Washita, Chief Black Kettle met "late into the morning hours of November 27" (Greene 2004, 109) with other leaders in his camp to ascertain what they should do. He had no promises for safety and was camped a good distance from the large groups of tribes down the Washita, an outcast from his own people. His was the westernmost camp. The next village east was the Arapaho camp, and east of this camp were the main body of Cheyennes and other tribes. A survivor of the Washita attack said later that after Sand Creek, Black Kettle "never camped with the main body of Cheyennes. He always pitched his village a distance from the main camp" (quoted in Greene, 104). No doubt remembering Sand Creek, Black Kettle's wife, Medicine Woman Later, agitated for an immediate move closer to the other tribes yet that night, but the foot-deep snow argued against a move before morning. The attack was upon them at dawn.

Many accounts have been written of the Washita Battle (actually, massacre) on the early morning of November 27, 1868, almost four years to the day after Sand Creek. Suffice it to say that it was a horrendous surprise to the little Cheyenne village buried in a foot of snow, and that this time Chief Black Kettle waved no U.S. or white flags. When the chief was warned by a woman running through the camp of the soldiers who were nearly upon them, he fired a shot from his rifle to awaken his sleeping village, mounted his iron-gray horse with Medicine Woman Later, and tried to ford the stream to escape. The horse was shot and Black Kettle and his wife were killed. They fell off into the water, their horse still struggling to reach the other bank, where it died (Greene, 2004, 129).

Horrors abounded on the Washita that day, as described later by the survivors. The young girl Moving Behind remarked on a dark figure lying on a hill, the body of a woman with child, her belly cut open (Greene, 2004, 130). "There, as the people fell at the hands of the troopers, one woman, in a helpless rage, stood up with her baby, held it out in an outstretched arm, and with the other drew a knife and fatally stabbed the infant—erroneously believed by the soldiers to be a white child. She then plunged the blade into her own chest in suicide" (Greene, 2004, 131). Horrible too, were the deaths of ponies the soldiers shot in waves:

> Moving Behind and her aunt, Corn Stalk Woman, still hidden in the grass south of the village, watched and waited as the ponies ran by, many of them wounded and moaning loudly "just like human beings" as the soldiers drove them to the killing place. "The snow on the whole bend of the river was made red with blood," recalled another woman. Later, they watched as the regiment pulled away across the Washita, headed toward the lower camps. The women then mounted and went to the spot near the

river where Black Kettle and his wife had fallen. They saw the bodies of the chief and his wife submerged beneath the surface, along with that of the horse they had been riding. Some of the men dragged the Indians' bodies to the shore and placed them on a blanket. The party then moved on, encountering the corpses of other dead tribesmen. "We would stop and look at the bodies, and mention their names," recalled Moving Behind. (Greene 2004, 135)

Just before her death in 1937, the fourteen-year-old girl, Moving Behind, was interviewed by Theodore Ediger for the details she remembered many years later. Theodore Ediger was the son of the Mennonite missionary to the Red Moon congregation, J. B. Ediger, and a correspondent for the Associated Press. The young girl Moving Behind had lived with her aunt, Corn Stalk Woman, who camped near Black Kettle. When the attack occurred, Moving Behind was rushed out of camp by her aunt, through the red fire of the shots in the early morning darkness and near a hill's steep path, hidden in tall red grass. There they stayed, repeatedly raising themselves to see the battle and its atrocities. They watched as the soldiers forced the Indian women to accompany them on foot, on horseback, and in wagons. They watched the soldiers drive the Indian ponies toward the bottoms, where they shot them.

When they finally realized that the soldiers had gone on, they came out of hiding, gathering with others. Moving Behind recalled that there was talk of chasing after the departing soldiers to shoot at them, but the Indians feared that they would hit the women they had captured.

Moving Behind recounted how the little party of survivors got onto ponies and rode down to the river's sharp curve, where they had often watered their ponies. There they found the bodies of Black Kettle and Medicine Woman Later in the water.

The circumstances of Chief Black Kettle's burial are disputed. The youth Magpie reported that "the day after the attack, he and several women pulled Black Kettle's body from the Washita and carried it to a sandy knoll, where the women debated over the place to inter the remains" (Greene 2004, 166-167). Another source argued that the chief's body was partly devoured by wolves before it could be placed in the fork of a tree (Greene 2004, 167). Custer's forces had marched away with more than fifty captives—women and children; forty men lay dead on the Washita alongside twelve women and six children.

Over the years, the site would be combed and scavenged, the ponies' bones plucked from the earth and sold for fertilizer. Nearly a quarter century later, when the Cheyenne reservation was divided into 160-acre allotments according to the Dawes Act, as Chief Hart notes when he reviews this history, "No Cheyenne chose the Washita site."

FOUR

CORN STALK

*I*n everything that I do I give thanks to the God who gave life to every-one—who created all things. His Greatness is manifested everywhere. I put God first in everything that I am going to do. [Here she meant that even in the practice of the rituals of the Indian religion, God is placed first, and it is He that is prayed to.] I will not do away with anything that is of the Indian. I am an Indian, and I do not know any English. Why should I forsake the life that I have known all my life. These things that the Indian has was given by God. . . .

—Corn Stalk, from a translated interview by her grandson, Samuel Hart for his paper, "Christianity and Indian Religion," in the course, "Our Christian Heritage," Bethel College, 1960.

Three years after the Washita attack on the Cheyennes, Lawrence Hart's paternal grandfather, John Peak Heart, was born, son to Afraid of Beavers, who had fought and survived on the Washita protecting his wife and his baby girl Walking Woman. John P. Hart, who had by then altered his name and its spelling, would marry Corn Stalk (Anna Reynolds) who was born in 1875, seven years after the attack on the Washita. Corn Stalk lived a long time: when she passed in 1975, she had seen 100 years of change for the Cheyenne people. A midwife, she helped lots of Cheyenne babies in the Red Moon tribe from their moth-ers' wombs into the lives they would lead in and around Hammon. In-deed, it was Corn Stalk who brought her grandson Lawrence into the world on a late February day in 1933. Because Jennie Hart, Lawrence's mother, was very ill after his birth, his grandmother, the midwife Corn Stalk, took Lawrence across the yard to her own house to care for him.

Lawrence remained with his grandparents until his parents realized that it was time for him to go to school. Then his parents, Homer and Jennie Hart, realizing that Oklahoma law required him to be in school as well as being strong advocates for education, made the necessary preparations to go across the yard and bring Lawrence home.

When Lawrence tells these stories, I recognize the care with which he describes the ceremony necessary to the act, the importance of "making the necessary preparations." These Cheyenne ceremonies mark events in time and *preserve* memory. Coming to take the young boy Lawrence home to begin his schooling was such an event. Today, as Lawrence recalls the event, he tells it carefully, deliberately. Clearly, Lawrence understood that something momentous was happening: His parents had arranged with his grandparents for an appointed time at which they will come across the yard with gifts to take him home, to thank his grandparents for their care for him. What were the gifts? He believes they would have been traditional Cheyenne gifts—a blanket or shawl, food items, perhaps the usual gifts of cloth for a ceremonial leave-taking. Lawrence would then move from his grandparents' home to live with his brothers and sisters in his parents' home.

By that time, however, in so many ways, the destiny of the six-year-old Cheyenne boy had been set. For example, he spoke only Cheyenne. Once, when I pressed Lawrence for what kind of stories he remembered Corn Stalk telling him, he mentioned bedtime stories and the stars. Traditional Cheyenne mythology referred to the Milky Way as the Cheyenne heaven, the place of the dead "where the Cheyennes chased buffalo, hunted game, played games, went to war, and lived in white lodges as they did before death" (Berthrong, *The Southern Cheyennes* 1963, 51). His grandfather too "kept back" this grandson to be instructed in Cheyenne ways.

When I stood before Corn Stalk's grave in the little Red Moon country cemetery not far from Hammon, next to where the Red Moon Indian Mennonite Church used to be, hers was the largest, most beautifully cared-for plot and marker. She appears here as the matriarch of this village of the dead, her grave place centrally located as one enters the cemetery gates. As I stood before her plot I remembered that she was the midwife for this people; she rests here as a kind of axis mundi in this little circle—her grave a visual embodiment of the matriarchal elements of Cheyenne culture. The large stone reads:

Corn Stalk
Anna Reynolds Hart
1875-1975
The God of My Rock in
Him Will I Trust
II Samuel 22:3

Chief Hart has told me that the cemetery needs to be expanded, needs to be carefully marked for those buried there. In fact, the day we visited, I noted the tiny, almost unidentifiable markers of those ancestors so prominent to the Cheyenne story hidden in the long grass blowing in the sharp March wind: Afraid of Beavers 1843-1927 At Rest . . . High Chief Howling Water 1864-1925 . . . White Buffalo Woman.

One must kneel beside the tiny stone to read the years of Chief Red Moon, who settled these people in this place: 1812-1901. I know that the old chief reached nearly ninety years of age and paved the way for cooperation between Mennonites and Cheyennes on this site. One of the oldest graves is the child of the missionary H. J. Kliewer and his wife Christina, the child who died and was buried here in 1905. The child's grave is perhaps the only non-Indian site in the cemetery.

The cemetery grass around the graves was not cut but allowed to grow to its natural length, long grass waving in the wind between graves. Marked individually, families practiced distinct ways of commemoration, some using short posts, like sharpened pencils, others outlined in stones, some large, some small, the artifacts and markers never uniform but individual, some with pictures and memorabilia I had no way of understanding: a pair of work gloves, glass cherubs, a white hard hat. A young man's grave (1979-1997) was fenced in the short post corral which Chief Hart explained was built in the Northern Cheyenne tradition. Beside the grave marked with the name of Whiteskunk lay a crucifix, a teddy bear, and a Mardi Gras mask. There were many beaded crosses. The cross on "Taco" Richard Ridgebear's grave (a more recent death in 2001) was graced with sunglasses. Alongside such adornments, intimate feeling made public here, I suddenly felt myself an interloper.

The traditional Cheyenne way to bury their dead was "body extended full length with arms at the side, wrapped in skins and placed upon a scaffold or in a crotch of a tree, or covered with rocks on the ground, depending upon what was available" (Chalfant, *Cheyennes and Horse Soldiers* 1989, 313). Furthermore, the "deceased's favorite horse was shot and left at the grave site, along with his weapons, if a man, or if a woman, her utensils" (Chalfant, *Cheyennes and Horse Soldiers* 1989, 313). There was still present such individuality in the cemetery, objects I did not recognize, or perhaps memorabilia of a certain sport.

Corn Stalk's beautifully marked grave was ringed by stones and lovingly cared for by her daughter, Blanche Whiteshield, born herself in 1914; she has readied her own site nearby. Chief Hart believed the old lilac bushes were brought to the Kansas Mennonite settlements from Persia, then brought here by the Mennonite missionaries.

Anna Reynolds Hart, 1875-1975. Born in the decade after Black Kettle's demise on the Washita, Corn Stalk outlived by many years Lawrence's own mother, Jennie Hart, as well as many of the babies she had delivered. Both these women's stones are substantially larger than their more prominent husbands' stones. Corn Stalk, the Hart family matriarch, lived to give Cheyenne names to all three of Lawrence and Betty's children.

Once, when explaining to me the matriarchal elements of Cheyenne family life, Betty smiled and noted that when Lawrence made the decision to continue his studies at Associated Mennonite Biblical Seminaries in Elkhart, Indiana, several years after Lawrence and Betty were married, she guessed he probably talked with Corn Stalk about that decision even before he spoke with Betty! He would have had to discuss his decision with Corn Stalk in Cheyenne, for she never learned to speak English. But of course it would be only right that he speak to her in the language she had taught this grandson as his first language.

Betty, a Kansan of German Mennonite background, remembers the day she was first taken to meet Corn Stalk before she married Lawrence. Trying to be the good prospective granddaughter-in-law, Betty admired aloud the moccasins Corn Stalk was beading in her home that Sunday afternoon. Sometime later when Corn Stalk gave the moccasins to her, Betty protested to Corn Stalk's daughters, who replied, "Well, you asked for them." Betty's admiration had been a signal to the old woman that the moccasins should become a gift (Betty Hart Interview, June 17, 2003).

For many years during their lives on the Plains, the Cheyenne women were in charge of camp life, encouraging the men to complete their necessary duties but certainly letting them know when their plans seemed unwise (Berthrong, *Southern Cheyennes* 1963, 36). For example, there are numerous accounts of how Black Kettle's wife, Medicine Woman Later, filled with fear and trepidation after her husband had been refused protection by the U.S. Government, demanded angrily the night before that fateful morning in 1868 along the Washita River that they move camp to somewhere less dangerous. Moving Behind, a survivor and witness to the battle, described the scene years later:

> Black Kettle's wife became very angry, and stood outside for a long time because they were unable to move that evening. She was disappointed. Sometimes your own feelings tell you things ahead; perhaps this was what that woman felt. She talked excitedly, and said, "I don't like this delay, we could have moved long ago. The Agent sent word for us to leave at once. It seems we are crazy and deaf, and cannot hear." (Ediger and Hoffman 1955, 138)

It was late. The night was cold. Moving the camp at that time seemed unwise. But there was authority and prescience in the words Moving Behind remembered Medicine Woman Later speaking that night.

Although Cheyenne women were not welcomed into tribal councils, the women's counsel was apparently heeded when the men went in. Thus, through their open persuasiveness with the men, "Cheyenne women carried their points about tribal concerns" (Berthrong, *Southern Cheyennes 1963*, 36).

Cheyenne women continue to practice many of the matriarchal strengths of the tribe today. Lawrence's Aunt Blanche Whiteshield, granddaughter of Afraid of Beavers, is one of a few select Cheyenne women to hold the sacred task of tepee making. According to Lawrence she is today the matriarch of their extended family. In this role, Blanche is in charge of naming. The traditional task of naming in the Cheyenne tribe is not simply a way of designating a Cheyenne name for the new person born to the tribe. It is also all about making the appropriate connections and, more than that, remembering family connections. Because naming is complicated—Lawrence pointed out to me in the cemetery two of his uncles who do not have the same family name—it was the matriarch's charge to help Cheyenne children know who their cousins are. For example, they must be apprised of which children may be their playmates but not love interests.

Chief Hart's family members all had major ceremonies when they were given the Cheyenne names they carry. These events are significant and ceremonial. They include careful deliberations with the oldest matriarch for information on which names are available and appropriate for the new child. A public announcement in a ceremony (frequently at the church) conveys the name chosen to the community. Thus Lawrence and Betty remember how significant it was that Corn Stalk lived long enough to bestow Cheyenne names on all their children.

In a panel discussion of the new exhibit on "Cheyenne Justice" at the Sovereignty Symposium in Oklahoma City in summer 2004, I heard Lawrence recall that the Cheyenne historian George Bird Grinnell liked to remind the Cheyenne people that Cheyenne women made the decisions: the men went into the tepee and talked all afternoon, but they knew very well themselves that the decisions had been made in discussion with their wives long before they came to the tent to begin deliberations! Lawrence wryly reinforced Grinnell's observations that day. Smiling, he remembered an adage he shared with the audience:

> We like to say,
> The Arapaho women walk four paces behind their men;
> Kiowa women side by side with their men;
> Cheyenne women walk all over their men.

Chief Hart consults his Aunt Blanche about decisions. She is the family memory, the history, the extended family's matriarch.

CHAPTER FIVE

ADOBE WALLS TO CARLISLE

" *They despised the hunters,*" *Chief Hart says of his ancestors who joined in the Battle at Adobe Walls, "who shot the animals, took the hides, and left the meat."*
—Hart, Interview March 5, 2003

Whatever we talk about in Chief Hart's past, it seems we always wend our way back to his grandfather, Chief John P. Hart. The name change, for example. The first time we talked about his grandfather, Lawrence remembered that his name had been changed from John Peak Heart, the name on his allotment, and Lawrence suspected it happened at Carlisle. Later that afternoon, Lawrence got his Carlisle alumni records to show me his grandfather's name on the roll at Carlisle Industrial School, Carlisle, Pennsylvania. How did he get there from Hammon, Oklahoma?

A good number of Cheyenne youth went to Carlisle. The story of the first Indian boarding school's existence actually began in 1874—the same year that shiploads of German Mennonites from Russia arrived in Kansas—and the last great buffalo herds still ran the Texas Panhandle. Lawrence became impassioned during the interview in which he recounted the old story of the bitter pill the Cheyenne people had to swallow as they watched the slaughter of these animals sacred to their way of life. I sensed a kind of blood rage as Chief Hart thought of the desecration of the beast which was everything to the Cheyennes, wiped out so quickly by the greedy buffalo hunters who came in and killed thousands of buffalo and left them rotting on the Plains, taking only their skins.

During Lawrence's days as a track athlete at Bethel College, buffalo barbecues were held by the Bethel Letter Club. They hosted as speakers well-known "big-name" athletes like the quarterback Bart Starr. Lawrence clearly relished telling me of his own part in that group of young men who went to a state game preserve in western Kansas near Garden City to shoot and butcher the buffalo for the celebration—perhaps his own longing to recapture something long lost to his people.

By 1874, the Cheyennes had long seen it coming. Sweet Medicine, their prophet, had predicted the arrival of the strangers. Now, the Cheyennes saw the impending death of a way of life in the massacre of the last great herds of buffalo in Texas. Weary of the desecration and angry, Cheyenne and Arapaho warriors joined the 1874 Battle of Adobe Walls fought by an outraged group of some 700 warriors from various tribes against a group of buffalo hunters in Texas who were slaughtering the remaining buffalo.

In spring 1874, merchants from Dodge City had followed the buffalo hunters to their camp in the Texas Panhandle and established the Adobe Walls outpost. It was built on the bounty of some two to three hundred buffalo hunters scouring the area. The winter just past had been particularly hard for the Cheyenne warriors, and they joined with the large band of Comanches, Kiowas, and Plains Apaches to attack Adobe Walls. Eventually, the tribes' warriors were turned back by the continuous firing of large armaments the hunters and merchants had brought with them to Texas. Angry and dissatisfied with their defeat, some of the warriors wreaked havoc on settlers along the way as they returned home to their tribal camps.

The U.S. military then made a decision to implement a tactic not practiced before. They decided it was time to herd together the warrior leadership and remove them from the Plains so they would be unable to continue to attack settlement groups. The U.S. Government would incarcerate the "hostiles." Subsequently, in April 1975, seventy-two warriors from the Cheyenne, Kiowa, Comanche, and Caddo Nations were rounded up and arrested (Viola 1998, 6).

How did the U.S. military determine who had been the leaders of the Adobe Walls attack? Chief Hart described the selection of warriors from among the Cheyennes as the result of a lineup. John Peak Heart would have been a three or four-year old, perhaps, playing at the feet of some of those chosen in the lineup. "You . . . you . . . and you, come along." Apparently, chiefs were given immunity if they would give up the "bad elements" among their tribe guilty of "horse stealing, arson, rape and murder" (Viola, 1998, 6). Surely, some of those chosen must have been warriors responsible for the incitement of violence on the Plains. But certainly many of those taken were randomly selected from a lineup to fill a quota from a certain tribe when a chief had refused to turn in his warriors, perhaps persons who actually had had no part in the Adobe Plains Battle.

More Cheyennes were taken than from any other tribe. Nearly half of the seventy-two prisoners were the thirty-three Cheyennes selected at least in part by a drunken Army officer who lined them up and took the eighteen men on the right side of the line, saying he would review his selections later, (Viola 1998, 6). Lawrence said the agent called for the Cheyenne men to come to the agency at Darlington. There the agent chose thirty-two men and one woman, chained them, and put them on a wagon to Fort Sill. Captain Richard Henry Pratt, who took charge of the captives, had, Lawrence believes, the typical view of Indians held by the military at that time—he would have shot them as savages. However, he had military orders to take them to Florida.

Those chosen were under the supervision of Captain Pratt, who had spent eight years at Fort Sill, sixty miles southeast of the Battle of the Washita where Black Kettle and his village were attacked not even a decade before. Pratt took his prisoners on a twenty-four-day journey from the Plains to Fort Marion Prison in St. Augustine, Florida, in an area then much frequented by New Englanders as a vacation spot. Enroute, at least two Cheyenne chiefs, Gray Beard and Lean Bear, perished in their attempts to escape or take their own lives. Crowds jeered the passing prisoners at rail stations when they passed through (Viola 1998, 8).

Somehow, however, over time and through his interactions with this group, Pratt was won over by them, and it became his passion to educate these Native warriors, to give them a chance to fit into the mainstream culture. Eventually, after their three-year incarceration, many in the Fort Marion group attended Pratt's special school for Indians at Carlisle, Pennsylvania, his answer to Indian resettlement. Lawrence's grandfather John P. Hart went to Pennsylvania, as did a number of others from among the Cheyenne groups in Oklahoma after this "pipeline for re-education" had been formed under the first superintendent, Captain Pratt.

John P. Hart would have gone to Carlisle to learn basic life skills, either sent by his parents or chosen to go study there. Lawrence believed it was there that his grandfather changed his name from John Peak Heart, as recorded on his allotment, to John P. Hart—the latter form a less "tribal" version he would use the rest of his life. Lawrence seems to lament the loss of the original name.

Warriors on the Plains had always used visual sketches to tell stories and to record events, for they did not write their languages. However, with the coming of the white settlers to the Plains, paper became available on which they could reproduce in drawings the important stories of life. The most readily available paper source that came to the Plains was the ledger book, a rather ironic and telling artifact in this clash of cultures where a business tool becomes the artisan's and historian's record. At Fort Marion, Pratt gave the prisoners drawing materials, and they sold sketchbooks to local tourists and collectors. But they also drew "pictographic letters to communicate with loved ones at home" (Viola 1998, 13). Today, these books of "ledger art" from Fort Marion as well as other sketches by Plains warriors, have become prized historical records and artistic artifacts of a people who did not write.

Making Medicine, one of the Cheyenne prisoners at Fort Marion whose artwork was prized for its scenes of Cheyenne life, was sent to divinity school in New York and became an Episcopal deacon. He changed his name to David Pendleton Oakerhater and eventually returned to Oklahoma, where he worked with the Episcopal church. In 1986, he was included in the calendar of saints of the Episcopal church (Viola, 17). After leaving Fort Marion, Oakerhater never drew again.

I was first introduced to ledger art through a display at Fort Supply in Oklahoma while on a tour along the Cheyenne Heritage Trail with Chief Hart as our guide. Gordon Yellowman Sr., an Arapaho chief and artist in the ledger style, is an authority on this work. He is married to Connie Hart, Lawrence and Betty's oldest daughter.

Above Chief Hart's desk in his office at the Cheyenne Cultural Center hangs a poster of Fort Marion, the old Spanish Fort, San Marcos. I remember well the afternoon during which we had been talking about the Adobe Walls attack, the lineup of Cheyennes, their terrible journey to

Fort Marion, and their incarceration in one of the oldest Spanish forts in the nation, now a national park. Suddenly, Lawrence rose from his chair and walked over to the poster of Fort Marion he has prominently positioned above his desk. It was a complete layout of the Fort.

"I went to Fort Marion to visit," Lawrence said. "And I sat outside in the sun a long time thinking of those Cheyennes incarcerated here. I had always wondered what might have inspired the Cheyenne men to do their art here so far from home." Lawrence recounted his experience then, sitting there in the sun, as a kind of visionary experience.

Suddenly, Lawrence explained, it came to him as he looked out from his bench in the sun at the Fort. The Fort is laid out in the Cheyenne traditional directions—with the cardinal points being "in the corners"—southeast, southwest, northwest, northeast. The four arrows related to these cardinal points are part of the Cheyenne tribal history dating back to Sweet Medicine, their spiritual guide, who gave them the arrows. The tribe's well-being was connected to the sacred keeping of these arrows, and Magpie had kept them carefully in a tepee on the land adjacent to the allotment on which Lawrence grew up. That day, on his visit to Fort Marion, sitting in the sun, Lawrence saw what the captive Cheyenne warriors must have seen, the cardinal points of the universe, the four arrow points, inspiration for art and renewal. In that moment he understood their inspiration, their creativity, their ability to survive, the sacred site in which they found themselves (Hart, Interview March 5, 2003).

The cardinal directions on the horizon as part of the Cheyenne cosmology permeate Chief Hart's orientation, his vision, his pragmatism. I watched him open ceremonies in Oklahoma City with movements in those directions. He has built the Cheyenne Cultural Center to lay out this universe—not the European north, east, south, and west, but east as the rising sun (*hesen*) somewhat south of European east; south (*sovon*) for warm spring winds and thunderstorms; west (*onxsovon*) where the moon rises; and north (*notam*) the source of winter weather (Moore 1996, 206). He turns to face these cardinal points in prayer, in seeking to know, in seeking the sacred.

SIX CHAPTER

CHIEF RED MOON AND REVEREND RODOLPHE PETTER

"Very well, we shall like to hear what we have never heard before."
—Chief Red Moon, in Petter n.d., 16

On my return visit to the Cheyenne Culture Center, I recalled the time I came with a group of students from Bethel College. In the tour he was giving, Chief Hart took the students to a corner he presented to them almost as if it were a sacred altar. In the corner was a sacred text, the copy of the dictionary and translation work of the linguist, pastor Rodolphe Petter.

On this day, as I enter the Cheyenne Cultural Center Education Building to continue with interviews, I walk past the row of computers on which the Cheyenne language work is done, on which children (and interested others) may learn Cheyenne. Lawrence's sister Lenora Holliman, a retired special education teacher, has developed a Cheyenne orthography more accessible for children than Petter's complex system. At the Cheyenne Cultural Center today, children click on a word and hear Holliman's pronunciation in Cheyenne (Miller 2001). I remember the day Lawrence spoke of Petter with the reverence one holds for a saint, for such he was in his passion to learn to speak, transcribe, and translate into the Cheyenne language the Scriptures he believed could transform their lives.

A gifted linguist who knew Greek and Latin, Petter as a youth in Switzerland had felt the call of God to mission work. After his brother had a dream in which he saw Rodolphe "in America preaching to some Indians" (Petter, n.d., 3), Petter followed this call relentlessly, learning German, then English, then Cheyenne, and devoting his life to the Cheyenne language and translation of Scriptures and hymns. He lived first among the Southern Cheyennes for his earliest work, then worked during his later years among the Northern Cheyennes.

Petter recounts in his "Reminiscences" his trip to Chief Red Moon's camp near Hammon, the encampment near the John P. Hart allotment where many years later Lawrence was born and spent much time in his youth absorbing Cheyenne tribal life. Petter, aware that many tribes in the West in the early 1890s were praying for an Indian savior, a messiah to deliver them from the miserable situation in which they found themselves, sensed a need among the Cheyenne tribe for vision in a world which had gone so wrong. He lamented that the missionaries were too slow with what the Cheyenne people needed:

> Had the Indians at that time had the gospel in their own language, I believe they would have eagerly accepted it and turned their back to their heathenism, for they were weary of it and groped for something better. Alas, missionaries were not ready with the knowledge of the Indian language, nor had they yet the needed Bible translations. (9).

Many years later, Lawrence does not speak of the Cheyenne need for a gospel of love in exactly the terms that Petter used, but he refers to the good news brought by the Mennonite missionaries in a way which resonates with Petter's early claims. When Lawrence speaks of "this Good News" brought by the Mennonite missionaries and educators, I hear it too as a concern for a people who were trapped, a dislocated people who longed for a vision and hope for the future. It was *their* good news, meant for them in their own language with their own right to interpret and respond.

Lawrence treats Petter as a kind of saint for the Cheyennes, I think, because he shares with Petter the belief that in their own language, the only language Lawrence knew until he began school, they could weigh thoughtfully the good news for themselves, its power and compatibility with their own religious history. Lawrence's attitude toward Petter seems to me not unlike that of an earlier chief, Red Moon, in his response to Petter's coming to his camp to ask the chief for the right to study Cheyenne and share the Scriptures.

Because Petter clearly believed that were the Cheyenne people only given the chance to hear the Scripture in their own tongue their lives would be transformed, he and his family lived in the Cheyenne camps. They listened, learned, translated, and shared their translations. There were no white settlers or towns where provisions could be had, Petter noted in his memoir. The Petter family carried along flour, bacon, potatoes, butter, and coffee, and they relied on the Cheyenne people's generosity for their meat. With regard to their access to game, Petter noted that he shot snipe so fat that they used the surplus for butter and to grease wagon wheels! (15).

In his memoir penned some forty-four years after his arrival at Darlington, Petter still recalled vividly his coming to Chief Red Moon's camp. He had been warned that this group "had nothing left for the white man, and would probably be quite unfriendly" (15). In fact, when he arrived at Chief Red Moon's lodge and requested of the old chief permission to erect his tent, the chief already knew of him, remarked on his ability to speak Cheyenne, and quickly sent his men to find deer or wild turkeys for their evening meal.

As the Petters sat eating their lunch encircled by curious Cheyenne children, the chief chided the children to let them eat in peace, for "a good Cheyenne should never gaze at somebody who is eating" (16). Petter also noted that it was the Cheyenne way to close an important gathering with "a meal—Indian bread, cooked dried berries, and meat with coffee. . . as symbol that the object of the meeting had been assimilated. This was the reason why for a number of years there was bread and coffee served at the close of our Sunday services" (19).

Chief Red Moon's Cheyenne hunters soon brought venison back to camp and continued to provide the Petters with firewood, water, and meat. The next morning Chief Red Moon came to the Petters' campsite to discuss with them why they had come. Petter explained that he had come from far away to bring to the Cheyenne tribe the message of God in their own language. Red Moon seemed interested, "Very well, we shall like to hear what we have never heard before" (16). He arranged for a meeting that night. Petter waxed eloquent as he shared his memory of that experience:

I read to them selected Bible messages which I had prepared with the help of Whiteshield, also explaining to the assembled Indians the purpose of our mission work among them. How eagerly and respectfully those men listened; Round about us the trees for walls, above us the starred sky between the branches, before us the squatting Indians in the firelight. I prayed in my heart that God's star might illuminate their hearts and lives. Today, forty-four years since then, stands not far from that place the Hammond mission station, where a Cheyenne Christian congregation was gathered through the faithful work of Missionary H. J. Kliewer and his companion. (16)

By Petter's account, Red Moon was impressed and asked Petter to tell them more. When Petter left Red Moon's village, the chief gave Petter his tobacco-pipe, made with the legbone of a deer, as a sign of friendship, and Petter reported at the writing of his memoir that he still had it (17).

During those years before Petter came to the Red Moon camp, Chief Red Moon's struggle for power against the Indian Agency at Darlington has been well-documented. As the Agency tried to disperse the tribes, spread them out over the reservation and break up the clustered camps, they ran into the power of the chiefs, Red Moon being one of the most recalcitrant. It was the power of the chiefs which prompted the Agency's move toward allotments, dispersing and re-settling Cheyenne families. The agents hoped that scattering the Cheyenne and Arapaho families on their own land would increase their self-reliance, but in that effort they needed to dethrone the chiefs: "Chieftainship is thus crushed and the dance drum is never heard in the farming districts," says Agent Williams around 1887 (Berthrong, *The Cheyenne and Arapaho Ordeal* 1976, 132).

The agents came up against Chief Red Moon again and again. First, he located his tribe on the westernmost part of the reservation and ran his own business of taxing cattlemen coming across the reservation. Initially, Red Moon would have nothing to do with the allotment system. "The recalcitrant bands under Old Crow, Young Whirlwind, Red Moon, and White Shield retreated to the western portion of the reservation, refusing to accept either their money or their lands" (Berthrong, 1976, 170). Red Moon bitterly opposed the sale of the reservation and certainly harassed the incoming settlers in his region. He would not send his band's children to the reservation schools. One could perhaps argue that when the linguist Rodolphe Petter came to Chief Red Moon as a white man might formerly have come to a chief—with an appeal to a chief to hear him—it was a recognition of the chief's power, not the common action of an agent from Darlington instructing him once again as to how his life would change.

On a March day 110 years later, I am going to Hammon to Red Moon country to visit the site of Lawrence's birthplace, the two small homes on the hill where his parents and grandparents lived. I will see where the Cheyenne camps lay in the valley near the river and visit the cemetery near where the church used to be.

In the cold wind which suddenly sweeps down over the Plains when we get to the cemetery, I feel again that day what I always feel in a cemetery: a huge sorrow for our loss of those who can no longer tell us their stories, a strong kinship with those who lived on these Plains before us, those with whom we are inextricably bound because we shared the land, because we continue to share a faith and a history.

CHAPTER SEVEN

DARLINGTON

Chief Red Moon opposed the sale of Indian land to the Government which would lead to allotments. Petter writes an account of the Chief's speech to his people during which he held a silver dollar in his lifted hands and said, "Do you want to exchange our land for this money? On this money is the picture of a bird. Birds never stay in one's hands, they fly away. The money you take for our land will fly out of your hands and with it the land of our fathers. Ye shall be homeless. You want money, money? And for it, give away our land? I stand against this."
—Petter, n.d., 17

Reverend Rodolphe Petter was not the first missionary to come to the Cheyenne and Arapaho tribes through the Mennonite Mission. To fulfill the call he had heard while still in Switzerland, the call to preach to the Indians, he came to this country to join an already ongoing enterprise of education and Christianization run by the Mennonites on the Plains. Though begun by the Mennonites, that enterprise had been requested by fellow pacifists of another denomination, the Quakers.

When President Ulysses S. Grant was elected in 1869, many in the United States were outraged by the U.S. Army's treatment of the tribes on the Plains. President Grant appointed a Seneca tribesman and Quaker, Colonel Ely Parker, as commissioner of Indian affairs (Hoig, *Fort Reno* 2000, 1). "Iowa Quaker Brinton Darlington was named as agent for the Cheyenne and Arapaho Indians who had been assigned a reservation in Indian Territory by the Treaty of Medicine Lodge of 1867" (Hoig, *Ft. Reno 2000*, 1).

At sixty-five, Brinton Darlington was already aging, and he really had nothing but his Quaker convictions to recommend him for the post: "Darlington had never met a Plains Indian, spoke neither the Cheyenne nor Arapaho language, and knew nothing of their culture or history" (Hoig, *Ft. Reno* 2000, 2). But Darlington would become a kind of local hero for the Cheyenne and Arapaho people, and his name would become known throughout the Mennonite world by virtue of being attached to a station and boarding school that drew numerous young Mennonite workers who became prominent leaders in denominational work.

Brinton Darlington bought a wagon and supplies in Lawrence, Kansas, the end of the railroad line, and headed for Oklahoma and the site where he was to serve as Indian agent. He and his son-in-law built cabins at the appointed site and waited for the Cheyenne and Arapaho tribes to show up. However, the tribes were still located around the Camp Supply area where they had moved after the Washita massacre, and they had no intention of moving from there. In response, Darlington went to find the tribes, moving to Camp Supply to work with the Cheyenne and Arapaho people, trying to learn his responsibilities and exert his will to get rid of some of the tribes' victimizers: "white horse thieves, whiskey runners, and unprincipled traders from Kansas" (Hoig, *Fort Reno* 2000, 6).

A convention of Quaker officials, including Brinton Darlington along with various representatives of various tribes, first met on the eventual Darlington site in 1870. Commissioner Parker sent a letter to the gathering, asking the tribes to "remain at peace, take up the pursuit of agriculture, and accept education for their young" (Hoig, *Ft. Reno* 2000, 6). Speeches were made at the convention offering the Quaker point of view, which abhorred war. Stone Calf, the only Cheyenne chief in attendance, agreed to settle down and take up farming. Thereafter, most of the Cheyenne and Arapaho people encamped near Camp Supply did follow Darlington to the new site. "Now began the business of erecting the physical structure of a new agency—houses in which to live, warehouses for the storage of annuity goods, sheds, fences, stables, blacksmith shop, commissary, and eventually a schoolhouse" (Hoig, *Ft. Reno* 2000, 9). A sawmill was installed, bringing equipment from Abilene by mule train (10). Little by little, what became known as Darlington Agency was being founded on the North Canadian River.

Almost immediately, schools were built to begin educating the Indian children. Darlington tried his best to intervene on behalf of the Cheyenne and Arapaho people for food, clothing, and equipment. The reports on his work were positive. He arranged for a delegation of mostly Cheyenne and Arapaho chiefs to visit Washington for the cause of peace. Things seemed to be going well; the Darlington appointment appeared to be acceptable to both sides. At a meeting of Quaker agents in Lawrence, Kansas late in 1871, they reported "the peaceable conduct and apparent intentions of the Cheyennes and Arrapahoes (sic) and other tribes recently roaming over the plains" (Hoig, *Ft. Reno* 2000, 12). However, by the following May the gentle, much-beloved Darlington was dead, having served only three years in his post.

A huge crowd of Cheyenne and Arapaho people attended Darlington's funeral, and many of the chiefs accompanied his body to its gravesite in the sand hills "where he was interred, Quaker fashion, without a marker" (Hoig, *Ft. Reno* 2000, 13). His son would later come and move his body to a knoll overlook and place a marker over it.

When the new Quaker agent, John D. Miles, arrived at Darlington, the Arapaho people were somewhat settled, but the Cheyennes were not there. During the fall of 1872, the Cheyennes had gone west to hunt buffalo. Meanwhile, commercial intrusions were happening all around the reservation: Cattle were being driven across the west end, surveyors were on the east end, and a stage line and mail route between Wichita, Kansas and Gainesville, Texas ran by the Darlington Agency (Hoig, *Ft. Reno* 2000, 18-19). The mail route had stations every twelve to fifteen miles for stocking horses and supplies over the 240-mile route. There were frequent clashes between Indians and whites.

Within the Cheyenne tribe, as there had been for many years, the old chiefs argued for peace and the young bucks threatened the peace. Stone Calf refused to attend his tribe's annual Sun Dance, fearing that peace would be threatened. In retaliation, the young warriors slashed his lodges and killed his horses (Hoig, *Ft. Reno* 2000, 21). Even natural forces conspired against peace. A long drought ruined crops for white settlers in Kansas, and they went after the buffalo to feed themselves.

These men, along with professional hunters, constituted an estimated two thousand or more non-tribesmen who were active in slaughtering buffalo on the western Plains of Kansas, Indian Territory, and the Texas Panhandle. Eastern markets paid from two to three dollars each for buffalo hides, and choice buffalo steaks cost one-and-a-half cents a pound in Kansas stores. It is believed that some 7.5 million buffalo were killed during the period of 1872-74 (Hoig, *Fort Reno* 2000, 22).

It is no wonder that the Cheyenne warriors went after these buffalo hunters at Adobe Walls in 1874. The friction in the Territories eventually grew into what became known as the Red River War, a punitive campaign conducted against the tribes by General Phil Sheridan. It ended in 1875 with surrenders at Darlington and the removal of "hostile elements" to Fort Marion, Florida.

EIGHT

THE MENNONITES
COME TO DARLINGTON

At first the regular Sunday services in the camp were held under the trees, in an arbor made of willows by the Indians. Later a large square tent was provided for these meetings, which could be heated when the weather became colder.

The morning and afternoon services were well attended. Old Chief Red Moon was nearly always present. When it was time for the people to gather, he asked the camp crier to call out the message. In a short time the men, followed by the women and children, came from their tepees and assembled quietly. They were respectful and attentive listeners even though the message came slowly, through an interpreter.
—Ruth C. Linscheid, "Henry J. Kliewer" 1959, 18-19

In his 1935 "Brief Survey of Missionary Activity in Oklahoma," G. A. Linscheid reported that the General Conference Mennonites began their work in 1880 by establishing boarding schools, first at Darlington, then later in 1883, in Cantonment. "After some years out-stations were opened here and there without schools but by the preaching of the word on Sundays and otherwise in camp visitations" (Linscheid, "Henry J. Kliewer" 1959, 1). Such an "out-station" was Hammon Indian Mennonite Church, with which the John P. Hart and Homer Hart families were closely associated for many years. Linscheid noted further that though the mission work began among the Arapaho people, the Arapaho language was not mastered, while Petter's work with the Cheyenne language was successful. Eventually Cheyenne stations outnumbered Arapaho posts five to one.

The two early boarding schools built by Mennonites lasted eighteen years. The Employee Records of the General Conference Mennonite Mission, Oklahoma record the first employee as S. S. Haury and Mrs. S. S. Haury nee Susie L. Hirschler, 1880-1883 at Darlington.

In J. H. Seger's *Cheyenne Transporter* article on June 25, 1882, we read this news:

> We visited the Agency Brickyard one day last week and found a well organized force of Indians busily engaged in making brick for the new Mennonite Mission, which is to be erected soon. [Darlington]. Scabby and Paee Man were doing the molding, for (*sic*) squaws the off bearing and two others detailed to fill the pits. From this, it can be seen that Indian labor is being used extensively in this art and they are fast becoming accurate and skillful in their work. (n.p.)

In 1883, the Haurys began work in Cantonment, an abandoned military post, and many of the employees of the General Conference Mennonite Mission are listed with terms of service at both Darlington and Cantonment. Reviewing these early employee records at the Cheyenne Cultural Center reveals a list of nearly 100 names of employees who served terms in Darlington and Cantonment between the years 1880-1900. In the column titled "Later Occupation," as recorded by Mrs. G. A. Linscheid, who kept these records, one finds physicians, ministers, ranchers, farmers, homemakers, college presidents—who scattered after their service at Darlington and Cantonment across the country to settle in Ohio, Pennsylvania, Kansas, Nebraska, and Oklahoma as well as farther west in California and Washington.

The Mennonites found their work with the Cheyenne and Arapaho people much more difficult when tribal life was essentially splintered and camp life abolished after the people were placed on allotments. This made it much harder for the Mennonite missionaries to stay in touch with the large groups of Cheyennes: "To visit the Indians the missionary must drive many miles and frequently not find any one at home. The Indians, too, with but few exceptions have to drive a long way to come to the churches" (G. A. Linscheid, "Brief Survey" 1935, 2). Breaking up the camps and spreading the people on individual allotments clearly affected the tribal ability to stay together as well as the work of the Mennonite missionaries.

Linscheid was further troubled, in his 1935 assessment, by the toll the new religious cult had taken. This indigenous movement he described as

> a conglomeration and adaptation of rites, customs, and tenets of various religious beliefs, even including certain phases of the Christian religion, but is based upon the use of the 'peyote'—a cactus plant—either as deity itself or as a means of approach to the deity and of securing pleasure and health of the body. (Linscheid, "Brief Survey" 1935, 2)

Lawrence Hart was two when Linscheid detailed in his report six church buildings (five Cheyenne, one Arapaho) which conducted Sunday services, three missionary families and six natives who assisted with the 600 Cheyenne/Arapaho persons who had been received into church membership. Among those present and living in 1935 were 300 people.

Anthropologist John Moore, who has studied, lived with, and written extensively about the Cheyenne people, comments on the missionary expectation that Cheyenne people embrace Christianity to the exclusion of their own faith.

> The attitude of Cheyennes toward Christianity has always frustrated Christian missionaries. . . . Cheyennes in general have never felt that religious belief should be exclusive, and while many have been ready to embrace Christianity, they have not wanted to give up their traditional beliefs or ceremonies. That is, Christianity has been perceived as merely an additional source of power from Maheo, with Jesus serving in the role of an anthropomorphic spirit. Of course the missionaries wanted the Cheyennes to embrace Christianity exclusively, and not only that, to embrace some denomination exclusively. Beginning with the Mennonites, missionaries have condemned traditional beliefs as devil worship, and have felt betrayed if Cheyennes attended church on Sunday and a peyote meeting or a traditional ceremony later in the week. But most Cheyennes maintain the attitude that if participating in one religion is good, then participating in two or three religions is even better, so that a person can collect blessings from Maheo through several sources. (1996, 273-274)

What is clear to a contempoary student of Cheyenne history and culture is that the Cheyenne people had their own religion, strong values, and a system of tribal government before the Mennonites came to share their good news. One can contrast, for example, the mission experiences with the Comanche tribe. Marvin Kroeker, who has written the story of the Mennonite Brethren mission to the Comanches in southwestern Oklahoma in the persons of A. J. and Magdalena Becker, noted that the Comanches "have been identified as among the least religious of all the western Indians. They had no dogma, no priestly class, no organized religious system" (1997, 5). The Cheyennes, as scholars have repeatedly noted, were people with a long tradition of religious faith and values, of very careful religious practices and understandings. They were not in need of a religion or a denomination to fill the void. Rather, one can see how they might have seen the wisdom of integrating Christian elements and their own traditional practices in the Native American church, for example, to live in the new times that had come to them.

Indeed, Hart continues to this day to take every opportunity to educate the public regarding his people's rich religious and political heritage. In a 2000 address at the Washita Symposium titled "Lifeways of The People," he challenged early French clerics who found the Indians without religion, political system, or a code of law. He noted again, as he did in his commencement address at Bethel College, how amid battle in 1868 the Cheyenne people held their annual Sun Dance, their highest religious ceremony, along Walnut Creek. He described the political system—the male societies, the council of forty-four peace chiefs that has long made consensus decisions for the tribe. He noted the jurisprudence task of the chiefs. He described the matrilineal descent in the family system; still today he recognizes the matriarch of his own family in Blanche White Shield, "a walking encyclopedia of The People's lifeways" ("Lifeways" 2000, 6). He described the sacred system of cardinal numbers, the ethical conduct and moral behavior set forth by the prophet Sweet Medicine hundreds of years ago. He cited the role models who had shown the Cheyenne people how to live. He showed how women influenced the tribe, how the Cheyennes held to long-established family practices for internal relationships. Finally, he closed with the invocation which began the banquet, adding his own words:

> *Maheo*, God, ever watches over us.
> *Maheo nich shi va da min i. Maheo* is merciful to us.

We as The People are still here.
We as The People still practice sacred ceremonies.
We as The People still have our societies and special women.
For those of us who are peace chiefs of The People, we still
have a code that mandates we live highly ethical and moral lives.
("Lifeways" 2000, 15)

Indeed, if the Mennonite missionaries did not always understand
that they were asking the Cheyenne people to replace their long-held sacred systems, they also failed to recognize how their introduction of
Mennonite Germanic and capitalistic values—self-sufficiency and inde-
pendence, thriftiness, "laying up for future need"—were in direct conflict with long-held Cheyenne tribal values of social gathering versus in-
dependence; generosity and sharing; communal ethic versus individuality. Surely, however, the Mennonite interest in Cheyenne language and
education, the well-being of the Cheyenne community—even recordkeeping and news publication for keeping track of the tribe—was and
continues to be a major accomplishment of the interaction of the missionaries with the Cheyenne and Arapaho people. Such interest serves
Reverend Hart today in Oklahoma ministries, as he continues to shape,
mold, and integrate Mennonite theology and Cheyenne religion.

When I read the early publications of the missionary era, *The
Cheyenne and Arapaho Sword* and *The Cheyenne and Arapaho Messenger*,
both published by the Mennonite missionaries to offer news from the
various mission sites, I quickly recognized myself as a reader one hundred years after their publication. Of course, I was struck by the patronizing and propagandistic tone used in addressing the readership. "Work
hard today, or tomorrow you may die!" was one general theme, along
with admonitions against laziness, visiting when one should be staying
on the farm and taking care of business, promoting church attendance,
and keeping the children in school. The themes were those one might
expect from mission publications. But the publications also served as a
news network (and today a historical record!), noted the accomplish-
ments of tribal members, revealed the workings of a community, and
helped the missionaries to serve as liaisons for the Cheyenne and Arapaho tribes.

Frequently, the missionaries were also intercessors against government policy and encroachment. And they did not forget in their zeal for
Christianization the reason they first came to the Cheyenne and Ara-

paho peoples—to help promote education. They emphasized education, visited the schools, made contacts for further education for interested tribal members, and visited their church members when they were away at schools.

After Darlington and Cantonment, other mission stations were begun. In early spring of 1898, H. J. Kliewer was called by the mission board to be the first resident missionary to the Cheyenne Indians of the Red Moon Agency (Ruth C. Linscheid, "Henry J. Kliewer" 1959, 13). The contact was the newly built Red Moon School, where the Mennonite leaders talked with Superintendent Smith. They learned that the Red Moon Cheyennes were at the Howling Water Camp just north of the river. They took coffee and crackers for the meeting. Six years earlier Chief Red Moon had requested of Rodolphe Petter that someone come explain Maheo to them (14). Chief Red Moon had signaled approval of the mission project.

> The fat, genial Howling Water [Jennie Hart's father] offered his tepee to the visitors for the night. He moved his family to sleep with relatives. The robe covered boards which served for beds became quite hard before morning, but the men were grateful for shelter and for some semblance of privacy in this camp of red men, women, and children. Their hospitality even included breakfast the following morning. (Ruth C. Linscheid, "H. J. Kliewer" 1959, 15)

Kliewer first pitched a tent on the edge of the Red Moon camp and started his services—with the school children on Sunday and Wednesday evenings assisted by two Cheyenne interpreters, Robert Big Bear and Frank Hamilton, but he could see that he needed to study the Cheyenne language. He studied all the while searching out a mission station site. An early settler came and offered his claim a quarter of a mile west southwest of Red Moon School, 160 acres for $100. The mission board approved this purchase. Kliewer moved then to a dugout on the property.

When Kliewer asked that a house be built of local stone, large enough to serve as a temporary meeting place, the Alexanderwohl Church north of Newton, Kansas, collected $450 to start building the Red Moon Mission station. The house was apparently a wonder on the prairies: "a large, square, two-story stone house with gabled roof that looked to their prairie accustomed eyes like a palace" (Linscheid, "H.J.

Kliewer" 1959, 22). The north half was an assembly room. When Henry Kliewer married Christina Horsch, recently come from Bavaria, Germany, in a ceremony performed by Petter in 1899, they moved into the new home. The dedication ceremony and the Christian wedding of Mr. and Mrs. Charles and Josephine White Skunk commemorated the establishment of the Red Moon Mission (Linscheid, "H. J. Kliewer 1959, 23). The north half of the mission house was used for church purposes until the autumn 1902, when a newly built chapel could be dedicated.

In the brief history of the Hammon Mennonite Church written by Rev. H. J. Kliewer, (n.d., n.p.) he notes that the first four members of the Hammon Mennonite Indian Church were baptized by missionary linguist Rudolph Petter on February 11, 1906. The first one listed is Howlingwater, February 11, 1906, the "fat genial Howling Water" who gave up his tent for Kliewer when he arrived at Red Moon Camp—Hart's grandfather on his maternal side. His wife, Annie Howlingwater, who had been baptized elsewhere, was received into the church by letter in April, two months later.

In her biography of her father, Ruth Kliewer Linscheid describes how, as missionary Henry Kliewer was building the Hammon Mission, the old chief, Red Moon, became ill. Kliewer visited him often, repeatedly praying with him and asking the old chief to convert to Christianity. In his last days, Chief Red Moon called Kliewer to come to him. Kliewer found him "sitting on a mat, straight and dignified despite his illness. His best blanket was draped about his shoulders, and his still black braids were neatly combed and greased" (*Red Moon 1973*, 93). Chief Red Moon announced that he had come to his end, that he was too old to travel the Jesus road, but that he wanted to bless Kliewer's work and encourage the younger ones to follow the Jesus road. Taking the ceremonial pipe, Chief Red Moon, who had been so recalcitrant with the Indian agents, gave to Missionary Kliewer his blessing and his name, "Red Moon," in the presence of other leaders. Finally, the old chief gave Missionary Kliewer his pipe as a symbol of authority: "Hereafter Cheyenne call you 'Ese-oxmaasz.' Will know you are leader" (94). Apparently, Kliewer was powerfully moved and had to leave the room.

Chief Red Moon tried to make a farewell journey to Cantonment but had to be returned home unconscious in his wagon. He died on July 11, 1901, at nearly ninety years. His grave was the fifteenth in the mission cemetery, according to Linscheid (*Red Moon* 1973, 94).

At the time of his funeral, many beautiful blankets and articles of clothing were placed both inside and on top of the rough, handmade casket, and buried. Food, in the best available dishes, was put at the head of the mound by the family to satisfy the spirit they believed would return. His best horse was killed and left nearby, so the spirit could ride to the happy-hunting-grounds (*Red Moon* 1973, 94-95).

In November 1901, H. J. Kliewer reported Red Moon's death in the *The Cheyenne and Arapahoe Sword*. He reported Red Moon's birthplace as near the Great Lakes. He detailed his wounds "received in battles against other Indian tribes. Several scars from arrow wounds and a large bullet under the skin of his breast, were proof of his narrow escape in a fight with the Ute Indians, about 40 years ago" ("Red Moon" 1901, n.p.). He told of Red Moon's battle against Custer's troops on the Washita, where Red Moon's brother had been killed. Of the Adobe Walls incident and subsequent Florida imprisonment of warriors, Kliewer noted,

> When they finally chose to send some of their leading chiefs to Florida in preference to being totally exterminated, they were called to Darlington and there a selection of the chief warriors was made and they were sent to Florida for ten years imprisonment. Red Moon did not happen to be present when the selection was made. (n.p.)

Noting that Red Moon was responsible for his Cheyenne band's choosing allotments along the Washita, Kliewer added that he believed Red Moon's "hatred against the whites seemed to be growing less every year. He was friendly disposed toward the mission work, which he showed by calling the Indians together for the meetings, and by giving the missionary his name and his pipe" (n.p.). Finally, Kliewer ended his obituary unwilling to determine the fate of Red Moon's soul: "He had frequently heard the word of God, but we are not able to tell whether or not he found salvation through Christ and we leave it to Him whose judgment is true and who will judge every one according to the light and thn (sic) opportunity that he had in life" (1901, n.p.).

An additional note in the *The Sword* reads as follows:

> Red Lodge, a brother of Red Moon, an old ex-chief, died at Salt Creek several weeks ago. He was a great friend of the Mission from its earliest days, and he was much grieved when the school at Darlington was discontinued. One by one the old fathers are passing away.

In 1906, the same year of the first baptisms and the formation of the Red Moon Mission Church, the first fall camp meeting was held. These must have been gala events. As Ruth C. Linscheid described them, they were great opportunities for socialization, lasting three or four days. The camp meetings were designed to try to "encourage the Indians to stay away from other tribal gatherings of a worldly nature" (*Red Moon* 1973, 118). They were formed to promote "growth in Christian living" and make new converts, but also to dispel the isolation and loneliness of individuals in a tribe which had been broken up by the allotment system.

The Cheyennes knew and loved camp life. They pitched tepees in the traditional way—a horseshoe shape open to the east—and built campfires, cooked, erected a big tent, and ate together as a group. The mission contributed some food, and the Cheyenne people contributed. "Usually a beef, or sometimes two, had been butchered by the Indians. This was cut in chunks and boiled in large pots over the open fires. It had a flavor all its own, half wild, half smoked, but tantalizing" (119). Lawrence remembers fondly this camp life. As we drove by the site of the camps, he remarked that he spent lots of time in his childhood in the camps, playing or staying with his grandparents. He still savored that day the rice with dried fruit and smelling the large tin cups of coffee.

Ruth C. Linscheid described at this very first camp meeting her father's need for assistance and his tapping the twelve-year-old Homer Hart, along with another twelve-year-old, John Heap of Birds, to pass out the song books which were the translation work of Reverend Petter. In this account she described Homer Hart as being especially interested in the language—"I must learn how the white people can make Cheyenne words from those mixed letters in the books" (*Red Moon* 1973, 119). This introduction to Homer Hart notes that he had learned to read and write English in the government school. "He quickly memorized the words and tunes, and sang with the others who had also committed them to memory. . . . determined in his heart that someday he would read those Cheyenne books" (*Red Moon* 1973, 120).

Linscheid described the Kliewer family's mobile home as an "eight by sixteen flat roofed cabin on heavy wheels" (*Red Moon* 1973, 121) with hinged tables, folding couch, and oilcloth covered packing box cupboards. These camping traditions remain in the Hart family campsite I visited. Lawrence adds a new piece of furniture each year at the annual Sun Dance. So, too, the smells of outdoor life continue to be a feature of camp life at the Sun Dance. "They liked the acrid aroma of the smoldering fires mixed with the horsy smell of tanning hides" (Linscheid, *Red Moon* 1973, 121).

Linscheid's chapter titled "Encouragements" features Lawrence's parents, Homer and Jennie Hart. First, she detailed the hard times for her missionary parents as pacifists during the first World War, their attempts to resist the movement of the Native American Church, and the flu epidemic which swept through the area in 1919. However, Homer Hart was Missionary Kliewer's "bright light." According to Linscheid, Homer had completed grade school at the Red Moon boarding school and continued his studies at Haskell Institute in Lawrence, where he was baptized by a Methodist minister in 1913. Kliewer wanted Homer Hart to be his Native helper and interpreter and met with him weekly for biblical training (Linscheid, *Red Moon* 1973, 162).

Homer Hart had begun the work he would do for forty years. At this writing, Homer Hart's son Lawrence has persevered more than forty years in working for church and tribe in Clinton, Oklahoma. Collectively, they have offered eighty years of funerals, eighty years of holding the tribe together in Cheyenne and Mennonite ceremonies begun so long ago.

NINE
CHAPTER

INDIAN BOARDING SCHOOLS

In spring 2004 I visited the Historic Carlisle Barracks on the campus of what is today the U.S. Army War College located near Carlisle, Pennsylvania. On this site Captain Richard Henry Pratt produced his experiment in the acculturation of Indian children during 1879-1918, and the Carlisle Industrial School became the prototype for Indian boarding schools across the U.S.

The security was tight on the campus of the U.S. Army War College; cars were searched from glove compartment to trunk and including the working parts. When finally allowed through the checkpoint, one is immediately confronted with 186 small graves and stones in neat rows in the perfectly kept cemetery, most of them the graves of Indian children who never returned from Carlisle to their parents. These graves are segregated from the children of military figures, and there are a number of unknown persons under white markers. The Indian children's graves have been moved here from another site on the campus. They are not forgotten: Shoes, ceremonial rings with ribbons, and coins lie on top of the stones.

Several of the buildings on the site of the former Carlisle Indian Boarding School were constructed by the Indian students who worked for their keep while attending. Otherwise, it is hard to find traces of the thirty-year history of the Indian Industrial School. I came away with the strong visual impression of the tiny white grave stones in rows, the markers placed for the dead children sent here by their parents in good faith. And I came away with notes copied into my book from the "museum" building, the little Hessian Powder Magazine Building erected in 1777 and now used to chronicle the history of this site through a revolutionary war, a civil war, and finally, the Carlisle Industrial School. The exhibit included the following short statement from an old guidebook: "1879-1918: Bureau of Indian Affairs used Carlisle Barracks for the experimental Carlisle Indian Industrial School whose founding premise was: 'The way to civilize an Indian is to get him into civilization; the way to keep him civilized is to let him stay.'"

Donald J. Berthrong documents the saga of Cheyenne and Arapaho trials with education in his account of *The Cheyenne and Arapaho Ordeal*, which covered the years 1875-1907. The reservation schools were always suspect for the inhabitants of the reservation. They were frequently used by Cheyenne and Arapaho families in a barter with the Indian Agency, jeopardizing the children's attendance. When things were going well between the Agency and the tribes, the children were placed in school. When the tribes were unhappy about something, they kept the children in the camps.

In autumn 1879, word was received at the Indian Agency at Darlington that the Cheyenne and Arapaho tribes could send twenty-five children to Carlisle. There they would join the youngest of the warriors who had been taken to Fort Marion and would now be educated for life in "civilized society" (Berthrong, *The Cheyenne and Arapaho Ordeal* 1976, 82). Local chiefs like Bull Bear, Big Horse, and Heap of Birds eagerly sent their children away to Carlisle. By 1880, Berthrong says, sixty-two boys and girls had been sent from the Darlington Agency (Berthrong, *Cheyenne and Arapaho Ordeal* 1976, 84).

That John P. Hart went to Carlisle indicates something of his family status and interest in education. Apparently, children who were sent to Carlisle usually could read and write and knew some arithmetic: "[d]uring the 1880's education of young Cheyennes and Arapahoes was sporadic and generally ineffective. . . . The safest procedure was to send the children to non-reservation schools, where they would be farther from the turmoils and conflicts of their people" (Berthrong, *Cheyenne and Arapaho Ordeal* 1976, 140). It was into this climate that the Mennonites came to run reservation schools.

The tribes have been criticized for sending their children off to school "either to be rid of them or to please the agent" (Berthrong 1976,

140). Berthrong argued that the Cheyennes were fearful of sending their children to the boarding schools, especially fearful that they would become ill. The agency at Darlington was critical of Carlisle for another reason—its inappropriate emphasis on "book learning" rather than manual labor. Certainly it was true that the students who returned from Carlisle could often not find appropriate jobs for the crafts in which they had been trained. By 1887, 180 students had been sent to Carlisle by the local agency. In that group, twenty-five had died, seventy-six were back on the reservation, and the rest were still at Carlisle or other non-reservation schools (Berthrong, *Cheyenne and Arapaho Ordeal* 1976, 140).

As to the appropriateness of the Carlisle education, "From the outset Carlisle selected its students from the families of the chiefs and leaders. These proud people would not accept manual or common farm labor under the most favorable conditions because of their heritage and status" (Berthrong, *Cheyenne and Arapaho Ordeal* 1976, 143). John P. Hart would have been in this group. Furthermore, John P. Hart's attendance at Carlisle fits with the fact that he was part of Chief Red Moon's band located near Hammon. Chiefs Red Moon and White Shield, locating themselves at the westernmost part of the agency, would never send their children to the reservation schools. They said they would send their children to school when school buildings were built closer to their camps (Berthrong, *Cheyenne and Arapaho Ordeal* 1976, 226).

Until 1898, when a school was finally authorized at Hammon, Red Moon held out against sending his group's children to the reservation school. He was stubborn about this even when rations were withheld from his tribe because of their failure to comply in sending their children. Red Moon appears to be one of the chiefs who refused to have his leadership eroded by the Darlington agency.

Lawrence does not know what his grandfather did upon his safe return from Carlisle, but as to eschewing farming after a Carlisle training, Lawrence recounts how hard both his grandfather and father worked on the farm which was their allotment. Though Berthrong chronicles the inability of the Darlington Agency to turn the Cheyenne and Arapaho tribes into farmers, Lawrence's family held on to their farm, lived successfully from their earnings, and bought good farm equipment which enabled them to help others. Perhaps they loved the earth. Arthur and Viola Friesen, missionaries to the Hammon area during Lawrence's youth, commented that so often when they drove onto the Hart farm,

Homer and Jennie Hart were in the garden working (Friesen 1981, n.p.).

John P. Hart would have been among those who chose and accepted his 160-acre allotment by 1892. After the allotments were made, dividing up the reservation's about 4.3 million acres, the Cheyenne and Arapaho tribes retained 529, 692 acres, about one-eighth of the former reservation size. Reserved for schools or educational purposes were 231,828 acres; 32,343 acres were set aside for the military and 3.5 million acres were ready to be given to homesteaders (Berthrong, *Cheyenne and Arapaho Ordeal* 1976, 175).

The educational data at the end of the nineteenth century show that of the 833 children listed, ten percent had attended non-agency schools like Carlisle, Haskell, and Chilocco, two percent were enrolled in schools supported by county governments in the Oklahoma Territory, and less than fifteen percent received more than a few years of primary schooling (Berthrong, *Cheyenne and Arapaho Ordeal* 1976, 230). That was the climate when Homer Hart found himself ready for school at age six in 1900, the year before Red Moon, the traditional chief, died.

Both of Lawrence's parents, Homer Hart and Jennie Howling Water, attended Indian boarding schools. Apparently by 1902 "there existed 25 federally supported, non-reservation boarding schools for American Indians across 15 states and territories with a total enrollment of 6,000 students" ("Challenges and Limitations" 2000, 1). "Carlisle curriculum emphasized vocational training for boys and domestic science for girls. In addition to reading, writing, and arithmetic, Carlisle students learned how to make harnesses, shoe horses, sew clothes, do laundry, and craft furniture and wagons" ("Challenges" 2000, 1). The children, even as young as age six, had to work hard.

Chilocco Indian School in the Oklahoma Territory, where Jennie Howling Water, Lawrence's mother attended, opened in 1884. It was the first vocational training school in Oklahoma and one of the early off-reservation boarding schools patterned after Carlisle. Chilocco remained in service nearly a hundred years. Unlike Haskell in Lawrence, Kansas, Chilocco never became a college. At Haskell, students were taught homemaking skills and trades, but at Chilocco, students learned agricultural skills, and the school was totally self-sufficient. Chilocco was located in northeastern Oklahoma near the Kansas/Oklahoma border. It was the practice of the Indian boarding schools to remove the Native children from their reservations where their acculturation could not be affected by their families' intervention. Chilocco was built to emphasize "English and industrial training for tribes whose education had been least provided for before the 1880's" (Lomawaima 1994, 9).

Cheyenne and Arapaho children had been recruited from the Darlington agency from the very beginning of the Chilocco experiment. "By 1906 Chilocco enrolled seven hundred students recruited from forty tribes" (Lomawaima 1994, 11). In 1910, when Jennie Howling Water might have been in attendance, fifty-two Cheyenne/Arapaho children were on the rolls at Chilocco. Unfortunately, few of these children actually graduated—from the years 1900-1909, the average number of graduates per year was fewer than ten (Lomawaima 1994, 10).

Chilocco emphasized agricultural education; indeed, by the time Jennie Howling Water was a student, "all the children in the school were assigned their own garden plot, and the boys from the fifth grade up were assigned small fields. Students left the school building at four in the afternoon with rakes and hoes to tend their gardens" (Lomawaima 1994, 17). One wonders whether Jennie Hart's lifelong interest in gardening began in student days at Chilocco. Homer and Jennie Hart met and began courting while she was at Chilocco and he was attending Haskell. Lawrence said his family believes they met at a football game.

Lawrence finds it curious that his parents Homer and Jennie Hart would later send their older children to boarding schools, while their younger children, Lawrence included, went to public schools. He offers an analysis about his parents' philosophy on schooling:

> I wonder if my parents were doing an experiment to determine how their children would turn out if some went off to Indian boarding school, others to public school. The first four went off to Haskell, where my father had gone. Sam, Ramona, and I, the three youngest, went to the public school. Lenora didn't finish at Haskell. During her senior year she came back to Hammon, became one of the first Cheyenne graduates of Hammon. Then later, when she became an educator, she finished her teaching career at Hammon as a reading specialist! (Hart, Interview March 5, 2003)

Actually, reports show that the largest bulge in attendance of tribal children at the off-reservation boarding schools had passed by the time

Lawrence was old enough to enroll:

> The 1890s through the 1930s were the heyday of the off-reserva-
> tion boarding schools, and the majority saw their highest enroll-
> ments during the 1930s as a result of the economic conditions of
> the Depression. In 1931, 29 percent of Indian children in school
> were in boarding schools. . . . Off-reservation boarding schools
> housed 15 percent of all Indian children in school. (Lomawaima
> 1994, 6)

The pattern of attendance at boarding schools in Lawrence's family
reflects a national trend responding to the economics of the times.

CHAPTER TEN

EARLY GEOGRAPHY

Grandfather John P. Hart and his sister, Walking Woman, chose good land along Quartermaster Creek. . . .
—Hart, Interview November 12, 2002

I had asked Lawrence to talk about the influence of place—the geography of his early youth. Lawrence began again with his grandfather, born in 1871, three years after the Washita Battle, to his great grandparents, Afraid of Beavers and Walking Woman. Both had survived the massacre of the village of Black Kettle.

The daughter also took the name of Walking Woman (it was customary at the time, Lawrence notes, for mother and daughter to use the same name). Most of the survivors of the Washita Battle took their allotted lands in and around Hammon in the Red Moon community.

Until the end of the reservation period in April 1892, the Cheyenne people could live anywhere they chose. But in 1892, according to the Dawes Act, allotments were given out in preparation for the 1892 land run. Thus, individual Cheyennes had to choose their allotted lands, quarter sections (the land had been surveyed and divided into sections and then quarters).

Lawrence's Grandfather John P. Hart chose an allotment five miles north of Hammon, bottom land along Quartermaster Creek, about half pasture land, and somewhat hilly. There he built his house and barn and other buildings on the west side of his allotment, in the middle of the 160-acre west boundary. And there Lawrence grew up. The creek was very near, and Lawrence spent time there with his cousins who lived just west. His grandfather's sister, Walking Woman, had the quarter section adjoining to the west. During those pre-school years, Lawrence remembers life as idyllic. The children played up and down the creek, knew the swimming holes and the best crossing spots. They played with others whose allotments were south.

Lawrence puzzled over the fact that the creek always seemed to flow, even in those hard dry times. At least that is how he remembered it. They swam, he recalled, and played with rope swings. Once, Lawrence nearly drowned. At about age five, he went into water well over his head, screamed for help, and an older cousin came out and led him back to safer ground. But I sensed that Lawrence had to think hard to come up with even that fairly normal childhood trauma when I questioned him, pressing him to remember the difficulties.

They also rode horses—west and south were two sets of families they knew, and he and his brother Sam often rode horseback over those three allotments. His father and grandfather farmed bottomland, wheat ground, grazed by cattle. They were located in the far west corner of Custer County; the western edge of Walking Woman's land was the county line. It was good land, Lawrence noted again, with pride.

Then an ancestral memory came back to him. He called it a "phenomenon." It came back as a childhood memory of forbiddance, and he treated it with respect. They might be out riding horse bareback, which Lawrence remembers they loved to do, but at times—and these times befell the children as complete mystery—they were not allowed to play.

It was related to the sacred arrows. Walking Woman's husband Magpie was the Keeper of the Sacred Arrows that Sweet Medicine had given to the Cheyenne people. During the 1930s and into the 1940s, Lawrence remembers, the custodian of those arrows kept the tepee. Magpie, a survivor of the Washita, tended to the arrows and said prayers in the morning and evening. A person of importance to the sacred heritage, he was supported by the Cheyenne people; they brought him food because he did not leave his watch.

To this day, Lawrence noted, Magpie is still seen as a Keeper who adhered to the strictness actually required, staying with the arrows. He was there virtually all the time. Since then, Lawrence notes, things have become more relaxed. Keepers will leave the tepee or perhaps allow another to care for the arrows or the sacred bundle. But in Lawrence's time, when others would come to pay a visit to Magpie and the sacred arrows, the children were asked to be quiet; they were not allowed outdoors to ride horse or swim in the creek, perhaps for a day at a time. They recognized that something sacred was happening, and they knew that they should respect that event.

The Keeper of the Medicine Arrows was the priest associated with this sacred ceremony of the Cheyennes. The two red arrows were buffalo arrows, for subsistence and safety; the other two were black, "man arrows," for securing victories over one's enemies. The Cheyennes took seriously the keeping of these arrows as a sacred trust. The Arrow Renewal ceremony, which Lawrence remembered from his childhood, was to keep the tribe safe or was sometimes enacted as a sacrifice or atonement. The ceremony could be requested during war or perhaps by an individual request (Berthrong 1963, 56-57).

In fact, the Pawnees had wrenched the arrows (always carried into battle by the Cheyennes as their most powerful medicine) from them in 1830 in a battle along the Platte River. Though they had long since made substitute arrows when they could not get them back from the Pawnees, they had tried repeatedly to negotiate for them; as late as 1866 Black Kettle was still negotiating with the Pawnees for the arrows (Berthrong 1963, 58). When the arrows were eventually recovered, the substitute arrows were placed on a high butte in the Black Hills (59). Much of the travail the Cheyennes experienced in those three decades on the Plains was attributed to the fact that they had lost their strongest medicine during those years. This is the tradition that Magpie protected on the land adjacent to the Hart family place when Lawrence was a child.

Those first six years that Lawrence lived with his grandparents, he recalls, were difficult times for everyone in Oklahoma. They felt the repercussions of the stock market crash. The terrible "Dirty Thirties" had left the effects of drought on his community and people. Many families left their farms. Lawrence recalled photographs of those conditions, houses buried in the blowing sand in western Oklahoma. He offered with pride that his father and grandfather were able to maintain their allotment, to successfully farm there, make a living on the land they had chosen. As I listened to Lawrence speak of the 1930s, I remembered how often I heard during my own childhood that Oklahoma land had been lost during those years on both sides of my family.

Lawrence remembered accompanying his grandfather on the wagon behind the team of horses used for farming, helping as he could or going along to visit neighbors. They had other animals, goats, cattle, chickens—for eggs and for meat. They got along. Lawrence's older brother Sam, a grade ahead of him in school, and Lawrence often accompanied their grandfather as he traveled about.

As he unfolded the memories of those early childhood times with his grandfather, I saw Lawrence's destiny unfolding. He lived with his grandparents, a generation closer to the Cheyenne traditions, and absorbed their language and customs. His home site was adjacent to the place where Magpie tended the sacred arrows. Those lessons of childhood we surely absorb into our very bones when we are asked to revere, to be in awe, to stay quiet, as he was asked to observe the holiness of visits to Magpie's sacred trust.

In this context Lawrence began to explain his grandfather John P. Hart's relationship to the Native American Church, formally established in 1918 in Oklahoma, but long practiced by various native tribes. In fact, Lawrence's grandfather became a missionary to the faith espoused in the Native American Church to spread the use of peyote and certain forms of worship that incorporate Christian as well as native traditions. The young Lawrence would make mission trips with his grandfather. Lawrence told this part of his history with relish, perhaps sensing that his own call comes in part from his grandfather's drive for peace.

> I recall as a young boy, five or six, my grandfather would go west during the summer months to the Four Corners area, Colorado, New Mexico, Arizona, Utah. You may know, many years ago, the Utes had been traditional enemies of the Cheyennes. My grandfather, made a peace chief about 1936, almost singlehandedly made peace with the Utes in and around Towaoc, Colorado. He had in those parts a friend, Walter Lopez. I would accompany him, south into northwestern New Mexico, northeastern Arizona, where he made converts to the Native American Church. I would go with him or stay in Towaoc with friends of the Lopez family, to play with the family while he conducted meetings with the Native American Church. (November 12, 2002)

Those early years with his grandfather form a framework to Lawrence's seventy years. Recently, Lawrence and Betty were having lunch with some elders from Towaoc, and Lawrence was told how he used to entertain older friends of his grandfather when he was only four or five years of age. One can imagine this grandfather showing off his grandson who traveled with him. The child Lawrence had a little demonstration prepared, apparently at his grandfather's request, something his grandfather's friends enjoyed, according to this elder who told the story. Lawrence would be asked to demonstrate how the Utes did their Sun Dance. He would dance forward to an imaginary center pole, moving forward from his original spot, forward and back, forward and back, demonstrating the posture and steps. Then he would be asked to demonstrate how the Cheyenne Sun Dance was performed. The little boy simply rose, assumed a stationary position, stayed in his spot and danced, as the Cheyennes do! Apparently, the Cheyenne and Ute audiences loved this childish demonstration of the differences between the tribes, laughed at the differences as performed by a child, and remembered it to tell Lawrence for the first time when he was over seventy years old!

When we first talked about his grandfather's influence, Lawrence chuckled to remember a clue regarding his grandfather's reputation he received from a scholar he encountered in recent years.

> One day I was flying from Oklahoma City and sat next to a Native American woman, a scholar named Dr. Carol Hampton. She was reviewing a book by Omar Stewart. We had a conversation. When she noted that I saw the title of the book she was reviewing, she asked, "What do you think of this book?"
>
> I said, "Well, if that book is well-researched, it will have in it somewhere the name of my grandfather, John Peak Heart." [The original spelling of his name was used by Stewart.] It was there in the index when she sought it out! Sometime later, I met a Navajo physician; I told him the story of my grandfather taking me to the Four Corners area. He told me that if the Native American Church people had saints like they do in the Catholic Church, your grandfather would be one of them. He went on to explain that to this day, when they erect a tepee for worship, behind the fire, opposite the door, they build the half-moon; it is careful [ritualistic] work, very well-done. When completed, a peyote button

is placed in the center. Still today, they call that the John Peak Heart half-moon, after my grandfather. (March 23, 2004)

Lawrence is clearly pleased with these affirmations of his grandfather's early peacemaking work, pleased at these unsolicited honors for a man he clearly respected, and surely, one on whom he modeled his own life.

When I finally ordered my own copy of Omer C. Stewart's *Peyote Religion: A History*, I had already made the trip which retraced Lawrence's journeys with his grandfather to the Four Corners area, to the Ute Mountain Ute Reservation at Towaoc, Colorado. Stewart says that Southern Cheyenne Peace Chief John Peak Heart came to Towaoc every summer as a missionary to the Ute, beginning about 1916 or 1917 (1987, 196), nearly the same time that his son, Homer Hart, who had been baptized by the Methodists while he was away at boarding school, was received into the Hammon Indian Mennonite Church. Grandfather John P. Hart stayed with his friend Walter Lopez, described as a "Towaoc shaman and sheepman" (Steward 1987, 196), but he conducted religious meetings in the Four Corners area.

Oklahoma was the cradle of peyotism, a religion which sprung out of the reservation model set up by the U.S. government. Stewart believes that bringing together various tribes for education purposes encouraged tribal leaders to band together for the practice of their old rituals, seeking tribal power and vision. Lawrence's grandfather, John P. Hart, who had been for a short time a student at Carlisle, was a good candidate for interest in the peyote religion. Those who especially gravitated toward the Native American Church were "young, newly educated Indians who found in it a form of Indian Christianity and often became its leaders. It was a ceremony they felt comfortable with, in which they could celebrate the Christian ideas they had recently learned at school in a setting that was familiar and indigenous" (Stewart 1987, 97).

Also, the Cheyenne tribe had the largest number of their tribe "sent up" to Fort Marion in Florida after the Adobe Walls attack in Texas. Four young Cheyenne warriors—Co-hoe, Howling Wolf, Roman Nose, and Little Chief—became prominent peyotists upon their return to Oklahoma. Perhaps these older Cheyenne men would also have been an influence on John P. Hart.

Though the Mennonite missionaries deplored the Cheyenne practices which mixed Christianity and peyotism in the Native American Church, it is easy to see their function as part of the traditional vision quest of Cheyenne religious practice. In fact, surely Hart's life lived as vision quest, his constant search for visionary life courses and restorative justice for his people, must be related to the profound influence of his grandfather's melding of Christianity and native practices in the Native American Church. Whether it be a pilgrimage to fast at Bear Butte (*Nowahwas*), participation in the Sun Dance, or "putting up" a ceremony in the Native American Church (Moore 1996, 232), each represents a desire for vision, understanding, connection to the sacred.

Though the rituals of the Native American Church differ, they include the incorporation of "Christian prayers with the eating of buds from the peyote cactus, which causes hallucinogenic visions" (Moore 1996, 233). Ceremonies include fire, water, singing, smoking, but begin with the illness or problem of the participants and end with the sharing of dreams and feasting, essential elements of Cheyenne ways of knowing (Moore 1996, 233).

When I asked Lawrence why his grandfather quit going to Towaoc, he shrugged and answered, "Perhaps he just got too old." He had certainly done a life's work. Stewart reports that John Peak Heart took his Half Moon ritual (known for its strict ceremonial correctness—the John Peak Heart Way) to the Utes before 1918 and continued until 1952, when he would have been seventy years old, visiting Towaoc every summer (1987, 294). His ritual instruction was also learned by Navajo leaders of Shiprock, who came to Oklahoma to study with him.

In her book about her Mennonite missionary father, pastor Henry J. Kliewer who worked with the Red Moon Mission at Hammon, Ruth Linscheid makes reference to the fact that Lawrence's father, Homer Hart, became at an early age an important lay minister with the Mennonite mission. Of special interest to her is the story of Homer's younger sister Lucy, who died of tuberculosis at age seventeen. Linscheid laments, "Little could be done to help her physically for her parents were strong believers in peyote" (1973, 163).

As Linscheid tells the story, there was a kind of showdown in the John P. Hart home between the medicine man visiting the household and Pastor Kliewer over Lucy's illness. Apparently, the Mennonite missionary won and Lucy was baptized three days before her death. Later the same year, Homer's mother Corn Stalk was baptized. Church records show that Chief John P. Hart too would be baptized some twenty-three years later in 1941. Around the time of Lucy's death, Chief

John P. Hart had begun his missionary work with the Utes, practicing his indigenous Christian rituals. He would continue that work for nearly a dozen years beyond his baptism. He died in 1958, about six years after his last visit to Colorado.

Lawrence spoke with pride of his grandfather's mission work with the Utes as significant peace work. He honors the fact that his grandfather's thirty-five-year mission was to the Utes, the traditional enemies of the Cheyennes. When I prepared to retrace Lawrence's journeys with his grandfather to the Ute Mountain Ute Tribal Headquarters at Towaoc, Lawrence instructed me to stop at Two Buttes in southeast Colorado at an unmarked Cheyenne sacred site.

There, according to the oral tradition relayed to Lawrence by his grandfather, Cheyenne warriors resisted an attack by enemy Ute warriors. The Cheyenne warriors were able to save themselves, remaining atop the Buttes, holding their enemies at bay until they gave up and left. In those years before 1940, Lawrence's grandfather, John P. Hart, stopped at the Two Buttes with him to pray enroute to Towaoc to minister to the once-enemy Utes. Years later Lawrence has stopped to pray there with his son, Nathan; he hopes that Nathan will take his son Micah to pray there also.

When I first spotted the Two Buttes in the distance, they did appear as some spot of grace for those legendary Cheyenne warriors, a sudden and strange jutting on the landscape where there is no unevenness. They simply rise out of pastureland, sunflowers, scrub piñon, and sagebrush. There is a gravel road nearby, but the buttes are enclosed in a fenced pasture. The day was cloudy. I took some time to look at the buttes and then returned to the highway. Two shafts of sun descended from the clouds to spotlight the buttes, a natural event which seemed to reinforce their sacred history. The Two Buttes lie on a north-south line. Driving straight west, as one looks back, the two appear to dissolve into one distant hill, clouded in fog.

When I traveled to Towaoc in July 2003, I wanted to make the trip into Colorado as my own pilgrimage for understanding something of the significance of this journey, if only the geography of it. Colorado, of course, was the Cheyenne homeland for some years before the tribe was eventually confined to Oklahoma. Sand Creek, that sacred, bloody ground for the Cheyenne people, is in Colorado. Lawrence had told me that their most sacred site is in South Dakota's Black Hills: Bear Butte,

Noavosse (The Good Mountain), where Sweet Medicine received the sacred arrows.

Cheyennes go to Bear Butte to pray and perform other sacred rituals. Another important site for the Cheyenne people is Devil's Tower, the site where they believe Sweet Medicine died. They call this site by several names, including "Bear's Lodge." In his dying days at Bear's Lodge, Sweet Medicine foretold the coming of the horse, the disappearance of the buffalo, and the end of the old ways. Like a Muslim might make a trip to Mecca, a Cheyenne would go to Bear Butte to feel the original terrain, to know somehow the old ways and feel the ancestral spirits.

The Cheyennes have had to move their "homeland" over time. Colorado was a homeland for the Cheyennes after they had become horse people. Colorado remains today horse terrain, "horse country." I saw that as I drove through Colorado past hundreds of horses on pastureland. I thought then of how important the horse is to Lawrence's story—for example, those 800 ponies at the Washita site whose dying moans represented the death of a way of life for the Cheyenne tribe. Without their horses Black Kettle's band of Cheyennes had become destitute, immobile, stuck.

History reports that a Cheyenne warrior's horse died with him alongside his burial place; that horse was part of his identity. I remembered that Lawrence's parents secured two horses to give away, one which he would ride the day he became a peace chief.

Sleeping Ute Mountain is the dominant geographic feature of the Ute Mountain Ute Reservation; it towers over the barren area which seems to grow nothing more than scruffy sagebrush. The "sleeping Ute" as a legendary figure is projected as an entire body—a prone body, a ridge. There must have been some wanderlust involved in John P. Hart's travels here, to New Mexico, elsewhere—one notation in the *Cheyenne and Arapaho Messenger* reported that John P. Hart and his wife Corn Stalk had gone to New Mexico to eat deer meat! (December 1938). It is easy to imagine the sense of freedom Grandfather John P. Hart must have loved, ranging over the Plains, moving over the terrain, covering ground, perhaps retaining some of the old Cheyenne migratory spirit, the old life.

In Towaoc, the Ute tribal center was closed. The tribal center and recreation center are versions of modern sports complexes, nothing like I imagined or like Walter Lopez and John P. Hart would have known. I could find no one, driving by the Towaoc Baptist Church, then past a large complex which dominates a small, desolate town: the Chief Ignacio Justice Center, Police Department, and Treatment Center, with horses pastured nearby. The town appeared completely unoccupied on this Saturday morning. I had imagined someone walking somewhere that I could talk to. I had imagined someone taking me to an old uncle who would take me to an old grandmother who knew Walter Lopez, who knew John P. Hart. But I saw no one, not even a dog.

So we went to the casino on the interstate nearby where activity abounds at ten on a Saturday morning. An old lady in tribal dress caused me to wonder if I should ask about Walter Lopez or Cheyenne Chief John P. Hart. But she was busy talking. Everyone was busy, some at machines, some talking earnestly in low voices, their faces close; they were doing business. I felt that I could not interrupt. Those in front of machines had their eyes glued, their hands occupied. No one looked up. No one noticed us.

It was a huge complex with a large restaurant. People were at work in the sparkling gift shop, and a beautiful Harley Davidson at the front door beckoned the tourist to buy the raffle tickets available to win it. Everything was bright lights, hubbub, activity. One very "tribal-looking" man with long braids was fixing a broken machine, its front sprawled open to wires and innards he was groping through. Suddenly, I did not want to talk to anyone; I just wanted out.

As I left, it hit me that this casino was probably an analogue, a modern-day Bent's Fort, that trading place where the Cheyennes met the encroaching culture. For me, the casino is a metaphor for trade, emblazoning the forced and emboldened cultural artifacts which draw a crowd, competition, and business. Bent's Fort was never a military post; it was always a trading post, though the military benefited from its being there. I was put off by the casino's showy artificiality. I felt regretful that this is the kind of space many people in this country use to interact with, observe, or reflect upon tribal ways and culture.

After I read Stewart's account of John P. Hart's work in the Native American Church, I began to see the event of Lawrence's parents coming to take him home from his grandfather's house across the yard, with all its ceremony, in a new light. No doubt his parents did want to see to it that Lawrence would start first grade at the local Quartermaster School. But one has only to read the missionary writing in *The Cheyenne and Arapaho Messenger* during those years to recognize why Homer and Jennie Hart might have felt that they should bring Lawrence home.

Lawrence's father Homer was a highly respected "Native Helper" to the Mennonite missionary Rev. J. B. Ediger during this period at the Hammon Church. While Homer and Jennie Hart lived on the same farm with his parents, Lawrence's parents must have had to consider the Mennonite missionaries' disapproval of the Native American Church. Ediger railed against Native practices in *The Messenger* and praised the work of the Harts, on their farm and in their church. Homer and Jennie Hart's family was a model Cheyenne family who complied. They were the first family to put up the mailbox so that they could receive *The Messenger*, the missionaries' communication with and about those involved in the church.

The Harts were active in the local faming organizations, winning prizes for their produce. Jennie Hart organized canning sessions in her home, providing leadership to the rest of the community and putting away food for the winter as the missionaries were constantly begging the Cheyenne people to do. For having the best garden in the district, the Harts won the prize of a pig. And the Harts shared their produce, especially with the missionaries. The Edigers thanked the Harts publicly in the *Messenger* for the wonderful roasting ears they found in their car.

Furthermore, Homer and Jennie Hart were tireless church workers. Homer often conducted services, attended training seminars, performed funerals, and of course, translated for the missionaries. Jennie taught Sunday school, decorated the church at Christmas, and organized the children's Christmas program. Jennie and the children were always mentioned in the *Messenger* for their memorization of the Christmas story, their sending in correct answers to the missionaries' Bible quiz questions. They were clearly the backbone of the Hammon church.

Meanwhile, in patronizing tones, Ediger chastised those who did not stay home and mind the farm, those who practiced strange native ways he disapproved of—sometimes in language that hardly hid his cynicism. Announcing by name the death of "one of our older Indians . . . after a long illness," Ediger noted that "his eyesight failed years ago while he went about 'blowing' on people, giving them what he called the holy spirit did not help his grouchy temper. We often have been sorry for his wife and hope she will soon be at her place again in our Sunday services" (June 1933).

I wondered what kind of pressures Homer Hart felt from Missionary Ediger over Chief John P. Hart's practice of the peyote religion and his travels to the surrounding states. I wondered whether Homer and Jennie Hart felt compelled to transfer their son Lawrence from his grandparents' home to their own Mennonite home.

No matter. Lawrence would follow his parents' teachings. He went to a Mennonite college and seminary. He became an important Mennonite minister and national leader. But the influence his grandparents had on him in those formative years was clearly indelible. He became the Cheyenne chief his grandfather had handpicked and nurtured him to be. He had been set on a course by age six. He recognized the power of the good news the missionaries brought without denying who he was as a Cheyenne or what it meant to be the leader of his people.

CHAPTER ELEVEN

ANCESTRAL HOME

On our way to Hammon we drove by the site of an old mission, red and stark like a Mexican ruin, beautiful against the blue sky. I felt again like I was in a different country.

The Oklahoma Mennonite Churches own the land, eighty acres now, and the gas well on which the cemetery stands. We meander on from the cemetery past the country site where the little Hammon Mennonite Church stood until it was moved into Hammon. Past the old church site, we head toward Hammon and the allotment Lawrence's family still owns.

Highway 33 takes one west into Hammon and on, west to the Black Kettle National Grassland surrounding the town of Cheyenne. We went north on Highway 33 onto a long curving drive that leads into the yard where two small houses still stand. It is a beautiful site with a great overlook. I remembered Lawrence's pride when he first told me of the land his father and his aunt chose for their allotments on Quartermaster Creek. They are located in the westernmost boundary of Custer County; in fact, his aunt's land lies on the boundary of Roger Mills County. Lawrence and his wife Betty were the last to live in the little house, more than forty years ago now. The two houses, the grandparents' and parents' homes, stand solid though now long unused. The window glass is gone and the interiors have collected time's castoffs and debris. Yet they give off an air of sturdy strength. Lawrence remarked, pointing to a tree, "Grandfather planted that one."

I realized as I stood on the John P. Hart family allotment that it had been more than a half century since Homer Hart waited for the first glimpse of his son Lawrence's flashlight as he walked home alone in the dark. When Homer saw that faint light, he made his way down the long drive in the dark to meet Lawrence at the highway and walk him home up the long driveway in the dark. Lawrence and his brother Sam loved walking from here to Quartermaster School in their early years; in the spring, it was so good to be outside.

As Lawrence described his school years, I had an image of him always on foot. He admitted that at times he and his brother Sam would go as far as the bridge, play there all day until school was out, then return home. They were close as brothers and close to their cousins, sometimes riding their horses to school where they tethered them alongside their cousins' horses. Lawrence remembered the fun times, galloping home in a wild race, losing their text books enroute.

It was when Lawrence was in his second year at Quartermaster that Lawrence believes their parents could afford two bicycles for Lawrence and Sam. They loved riding their bikes those two miles to school. In those days Highway 33 was just another gravel road, as Lawrence recalled. One day the highway department strung a cable traffic counter across that gravel road in front of the Hart home place to see whether the traffic merited paving the road which ran by their house. Homer Hart explained to the boys what the counter was all about, and they determined to take matters into their own hands to get the highway paved. They rode their bikes in circles over the counter time after time all afternoon.

Betty noted with a chuckle, as we left the Hart place to drive to Hammon along the highway that Lawrence and Sam Hart helped to get paved, that she had been told that on a Saturday a chicken might suddenly disappear from Lawrence's mother's flock. That would be because Sam and Lawrence nabbed one, sold it at the local store, and used their profit to go to the movies. What movies, I asked? Lone Ranger, Roy Rogers, Lawrence replied. Mostly Westerns.

The Cheyenne camps were located in Chief Ben Whiteshield's allotment, where Lawrence came to play and where local minister J. B. Ediger dressed as Santa Claus and came to hand out treats—Christmas peppernuts from the Women's Mission group at the Inman (Kan.) Mennonite Church.

The Cheyenne camps were Lawrence's playground, building a sense of tribal identity. He often stayed with his grandparents in their tent at the camps. "There were times as I was growing up with my biological parents, I'd get permission to go to the camps and stay. But usually they wanted me home for night" (March 4, 2004). He always walked. Lawrence said that his strongest childhood memory is walking, walking everywhere. It was safe then, he remembers, walking in the night.

The Community Hall in the center of Hammon was once an important place to gather. There were Indian dances, and Pete Finger Nails made their outfits. His brother led the singers. During the summer, Lawrence recalled, a fellow up the Washita got a contract to bring Cheyenne dancers to Gallup, New Mexico to the intertribal dances. He selected dancers, and Lawrence got to go several times. Albert Hoffman, the contractor for Gallup intertribal ceremonies, had hired a big eighteen wheeler, a cattle truck. Their group of dancers tarped the truck bed, put benches inside, and headed for Albuquerque. They stayed overnight at a park, in tents, or slept on the bed of the truck.

Lawrence appreciated the camaraderie and togetherness of those journeys. He expressed gratitude for people like Pete and Martha Finger Nails who served as sponsors for the younger dancers. Pete worked with the Cheyenne youth. He organized baseball teams. He helped the young kids develop pride in their abilities, in who they were. Lawrence smiled, "We had some good teams." He commented then on the wholesomeness of their fun. "I am grateful for this wholesome entertainment provided for me at an important time in my youth." I recognize how much of Lawrence's life has been and continues today to be devoted to Cheyenne youth.

When I asked probing questions of Lawrence about the curriculum he studied in high school, I expected some resentment that he was not taught in school what he has spent the rest of his life having to learn. Lawrence shrugged it off. He remembered studying Jamestown, the Colonies, the standard American history texts of the 1940s. I persisted, demanding to know what might have been useful to him in that education. Suddenly he recalled an eighth-grade health class which he deemed very significant. It helped him, he argued. He cared about his body and good health. Some of his cousins began using alcohol; some became addicted; some died. Lawrence was not tempted by alcohol. He credits that health class with having a powerful effect on him.

When I asked about leadership, whether he might have felt that he was being trained as a leader, he shrugged again. Finally, he remembered that he was usually a class officer, that he was senior class president. He was more talkative, however, about his contributions to journalism, his drawings, working late after school on the high school yearbook. He credited his Mennonite pastor, Arthur Friesen, for getting him and his brother Sam and Robert Standing Water to consider education beyond high school. He thinks his father Homer Hart probably saw to it that meetings with Friesen happened. It was not easy to get them to go on to college. Lawrence believes that Friesen was grooming them to become young leaders in the church.

As one enters the town of Hammon, what stands out for a first-time observer are the excellent school buildings in a tiny Oklahoma town, especially when contrasted with some of the homes which need repair. Lawrence has told me earlier that his high school burned, destroying pictures and records I wanted to see—his drawings, his journalism work. But this school I see in Hammon today is an amazingly modern and well-built campus, with impressive arts buildings and gymnasium, thanks to the gas boom of the early 1980s. The gas tax went to the schools. Lawrence's sister taught at Hammon for a time. But the population does not stay here in Hammon, a tired little town. Lawrence told me that in the last census northwest Oklahoma had lost so many people that the state lost a congressional seat.

As we left Hammon, I badgered Lawrence to try to get him to help me get all the dates straight—attendance at Quartermaster 1939-1942, finishing eighth grade in Hammon in 1948, high school 1948-1952. Lawrence patiently allowed me to probe the years with him, but he has no interest in the precise dates of his own life in the same way that he cares about the momentous dates of Sand Creek or the Washita Massacre. Likewise for his family tree. I sometimes felt like an intruder when I asked for clarification on the family tree. I finally realized that a family tree like my Germanic forbears treasure is not an appropriate way to see the extended family relationships and village life model that Lawrence values. He does, indeed, value the past, the stories, the people, the events—but recordkeeping for the sake of tracing lineage is a forced act, perhaps not fitting.

Left: *Chief John P. Hart, Lawrence Hart's paternal grand-father, one of four principal peace chiefs of the Cheyenne in traditional buckskin.* **Above:** *Original Haoenaom Station, Clinton mission established by Rev. M. M. Horsch, with parsonage and barn.* Grateful acknowledgment is made to the Lawrence and Betty Hart photo collection for permission to use all photos reproduced in this book, as well as to sources of some photos in the Hart collection credited for specific photos in the following pages.

Corn Stalk and Chief John P. Hart, Lawrence Hart's paternal grandparents.
Credit: Arthur Friesen

Homer and Jennie Hart family, about 1934: (left to right) Alvin, Sam, Lucy, Lenora, Christine in front, Homer, Jennie holding Lawrence.

Homer and Jennie Hart family on John P. Hart allotment; back row: Lucy, Alvin, Lenora; second row: Homer, Christine, Jennie holding Ramona; front row: Lawrence and Sam.

Above: *Jennie and Homer Hart, Lawrence Hart's parents.* Credit: Arthur Friesen

Below left: *Young Lawrence Hart photographed while traveling with Grandfather John P. Hart.* **Right:** *Arthur and Viola Friesen and Homer Hart beside Red Moon Mission Church.* Credit: Arthur Friesen

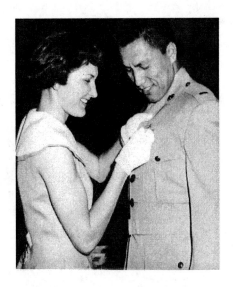

Above left: *Naval Aviation Cadet Lawrence Hart.* **Right:** *Betty pinning wings of gold on Lawrence after he completed flight training as jet pilot.*

Lawrence and Betty Hart Wedding, October 4, 1957, Bruderthal Mennonite Church, rural Hillsboro, Kansas

Above: *Lawrence Hart receiving final instructions at initiation ceremony to become a chief in tepee June 15, 1958; (left to right): Amos Hawk, Lawrence Hart, Jacob Allrunner, Felix Whiteshield.*

Left: *Lawrence Hart carries peace pipe bag walking toward tepee for peace chief initiation, June 15, 1958.*

Betty and Lawrence Hart (pastoral intern), Connie and Nathan in Reedley, California.
Credit: Arthur Friesen

Rev. Ralph Weber in commissioning service for Lawrence and Betty Hart at Hammon Church, formerly Red Moon Mission.

Lawrence Hart speaks at Laurelville Mennonite Retreat Center. Credit: Paul M. Schrock Photos, Harrisonburg, Virginia

Lawrence Hart with boys in anti-drug program, "The Circle Keepers."

Above: *Hart family at Evening Lions Club Park honor dance for Cristina, Miss Indian Oklahoma, 1987. Left to right: Connie, Cristina, Betty, Nathan, Lawrence.*

Below: *Cheyenne Cultural Center on Route 66*

Chief Lawrence Hart at the Washita Massacre Site.

Rev. Lawrence Hart with children around altar table Advent Sunday at Koinonia Church.

Lawrence Hart listens to family matriarch Blanche Whiteshield whisper the name in Cheyenne naming ceremony; left to right: Lawrence Hart, daughter Cristina, Blanche Hart Whiteshield holding Cristina's daughter Lexus.

CHAPTER THIRTEEN

THE COTTON FIELD DECISION

Hanging in my garage I have an old cotton scale that my mother gave me. I remember seeing it in our feedroom during my childhood, though I had no idea what it was. All the while I gathered wads of Oklahoma cotton field images in my head as my parents told cotton picking stories. Cotton fields and picking have always connected Oklahoma with the deeper South in my head, the South of *Uncle Tom's Cabin*, a book I read when very young. My mother, especially, talked about picking cotton as a child during the hard Depression years. When she told those stories, I learned that the seven children in her family considered cotton picking to be of paramount importance to the family welfare. I connected them to the Old South, these children who dragged 100-pound cotton sacks between the prickly rows of cotton to the scales and the wagon where they dumped the heavy sacks. I have never picked cotton, but I know that one's fingers bleed. It is this image from my mother that I bring to my own understanding of Lawrence Hart's cotton field decision.

During the fall, maybe October, Lawrence thought, the public schools at Hammon were dismissed for two weeks after consultation with local farmers. When the cotton was ready for picking, closing school allowed the school children to help. Their work and earnings helped their families buy shoes. Sometimes it was fun, picking alongside siblings, Lawrence recalled. "He rather liked the competition, the break from the classroom, the sweating in the sun," I thought as I heard him say it. It was probably different for him than for my mother.

Or maybe not. Once, when he found the work hard, dragging a heavy sack (the more pounds, the more money, he reminded me), Lawrence was so tired he simply had to stop. He lay back between the rows of cotton to just look up into the sky, watch for planes. What he was seeing, he explained to me, were U. S. Navy twin engine planes out of Hutchinson, Kansas, where there was a Naval Air Base, or perhaps nearby Clinton-Sherman Air Station. The planes were performing maneuvers in training flights (Hart, Interview June 17, 2003).

As he began to tell me this story, I had a sudden memory of an earlier time when I was with a group of students on the Cheyenne Heritage Trail with Chief Hart as our guide, and we were making a stopover at Fort Supply. An older man sidled up to Chief Hart, looked up at him with admiration and shook his hand, introducing himself. I was observing from another corner.

"Aren't you Lawrence Hart?" the older man asked him, rather reverentially, I thought. "I remember you. I remember when you were a fighter pilot, when you would come low and buzz our town. Yes, I remember that well." Lawrence nodded, ducked his head. He was being treated like an aging celebrity.

That day in in the cotton field, Lawrence made a decision. He would not always pick cotton. On training flights the twin-engine planes, trailing wires to sense radio transmissions, would come in low over where Lawrence lay in the cotton field. That day he looked up—and he wanted to fly. He remembers that then and there he wanted to leave the cotton fields. He vowed to apply himself, to stay healthy to fulfill that dream.

Indeed, his high school years were marked by that cotton field decision. He would not smoke. He would not drink, even when his cousins did. "I had this ambition," he says, "that if I stayed healthy, did well in school, I might have a chance" (June 17, 2003). What are the moments that separate out certain ones of us for a certain destiny? We have strange visions, imagining ourselves somewhere else. Some of these dreams last only until the end of the cotton row; others hang onto us, stick to us like the bolls of cotton which prick our fingers to the blood.

Lawrence mentioned his dream to one of his favorite teachers, a woman who told him it would require a lot to go into the military and become a pilot. Perhaps she meant to suggest, he acknowledged, that he had set his ambitions too high. He took it as a challenge, as a motivator.

And of course, there was once again the powerful influence of his grandfather, Chief John P. Hart. Those summers in his youth when he had gone with his grandfather to the Four Corners area near Towaoc, Colorado, where they would travel to the Ute Mountain Ute Reservation, Lawrence remembers as impressionable years during which he and his brother Sam played with friends in the mountains there. Just being with his grandfather, Lawrence says, just being near him, developing a close relationship with him, watching what he did and who he was, watching him interact with others, was a powerful influence on his life.

It must have been 1943 or 1944, Lawrence thinks, and he was probably ten or eleven that summer when the Navajo Marines—Privates Tso and Yazzie—each made a special trip to see his grandfather. When he looks back now, he understands that this visit to his grandfather, a Cheyenne chief, must have been crucial to the young Marines, since they gave up a couple of days' leave to come to Oklahoma to see and be blessed by him.

Lawrence was in his grandfather's house when each of them came, present while his grandfather blessed each man. He watched carefully, as any boy would have. The Marines were in top physical condition, "sharp," Lawrence remembers. They wore their uniforms, pressed shirts and trousers, shiny belts and shoes. In awe, Lawrence watched his grandfather light the cedar incense and brush each with an eagle wing, as they faced east. They went on then, to assignments in the Pacific theatre. But Lawrence never forgot them and always continued to wonder about them. He later learned their names—Chester Tso and William Yazzie; both were part of the Navajo code-talker contingent. Both men made it home safely. Lawrence believes his cotton field decision was related to that image, too, watching that blessing from his grandfather upon the Navajo soldiers, handsome and respectful, facing east.

Lawrence held on to the cotton field dream. He kept his body strong, fought off the temptations which would have distracted him. He even resisted the pacifist doctrine of the Mennonite college he attended for two years before he enlisted. He remembers today extensive interviews, tests at the Dallas Naval Air Station. And then he remembers his parents bringing him to Clinton to the airport where a two-seater, single-engine navy plane, an SNJ like he would fly in Basic Training, came to take Lawrence from the cotton fields and red soil of Oklahoma up into the air.

CHAPTER FOURTEEN

DOG SOLDIER DAYS

I was especially curious about Lawrence's military service. Somehow it did not fit for me. I knew that he was brought up as a Cheyenne, and of course there is a strong military tradition among the Cheyennes, as there is among other native tribes. But he was also raised a Mennonite. He attended church. He did not rebel. I presumed that he would have been taught to be a pacifist—although many young Mennonite men in Oklahoma went into the military during World War II.

My own father, an Oklahoma Mennonite, went into the Army as a non-combatant at the end of World War II. Because he spoke German, he was educated at Heidelberg University and served as an interpreter for the interrogation of German prisoners. My father died before I could really question him regarding how he came to this decision. His cousins who were age mates told me that he was encouraged by his uncles to go into the military to support his newly widowed mother and her two youngest children. I was curious as to what motivated Lawrence to enlist first with the Navy, where he took his training before he was commissioned in the United States Marine Corps.

For Lawrence, the Navy was an avenue, a route whereby he could fulfill a dream. It occurred to me that it represented a private dream, a secret goal, his own internal glowing ember and challenge. When he first told me about this stage in his life, he said he believed he was the first full-blooded Native American to make it as a jet fighter pilot. This burning challenge he had given himself held him in thrall and provided the earthly challenge he needed until his grandfather called again from the spirit world.

When I read about the early years of the great Cheyenne chiefs, I discovered that most great chiefs had a warrior period in their lives. In traditional Cheyenne tribal life, the military societies were the tribal police and disciplinarians. A young Cheyenne boy between the ages of thirteen and sixteen would be initiated into the military society of his choice or join his father's. There were several societies, as dictated by Sweet Medicine—the Wolf-Soldiers, Fox-Soldiers, Dog-Soldiers, Bull-Soldiers, Bowstrings. The Dog Soldiers, best known for their prowess in the battles on the Plains, were the most important and aggressive. They controlled the tribe.

Though his background was hard to reconstruct, the "great peacemaker" himself, Black Kettle, was purported to have been a great warrior in his youth (Hoig, *Peace Chiefs* 1980, 105). A great peace chief must have a conversion experience. Sweet Medicine instructs that a peace chief, though at one time a warrior, must take the peace pipe and smoke even if his son be killed in front of his tepee. This conversion experience is also part of Peace Chief Lawrence Hart's life.

Lawrence remembered that even though he knew about the Mennonite peace position from Arthur Friesen, his pastor during his high school years and the one who encouraged him to attend Bethel College, the peace position did not really make an impression on him until he learned more about it at Bethel College.

Certainly, not all of his encounters with the students he assumed to be pacifists at Bethel were positive. He still remembers observing an encounter which he found to be unjust. A bearded fellow—perhaps a Canadian or an Amishman—was asked by fellow students who took offense at the beard to shave his beard in those early years of the 1950s. He would not shave the beard, and the students continued to harass him. Lawrence witnessed an almost violent encounter when the students came and insisted that they would drag the bearded student out and force him to shave. The students who advocated physical force were stopped, but Lawrence was surprised by the hypocrisy of their supposed pacifism. How can you advocate for peace and behave violently with your neighbor?

Lawrence had, however, other positive experiences at Bethel related to advocacy for pacifism which he believes began to move him toward a life of peacemaking. Elmer Ediger gave chapel talks on the peace tradition which interested him. And there were ways he felt welcomed into Christian community despite his military position. One of his science professors at Bethel was a former Army ranger, which impressed him.

There was a certain ecumenical spirit of inclusion that helped Lawrence to conclude that he could be in the military and still be a Christian. To give an example, Lawrence tells the following story. After he had been on campus awhile, he realized that he needed a haircut. So he went downtown Newton to a barber. Lawrence sat down in the chair to wait his turn, but the barber asked what he wanted. When Lawrence told him, he retorted, "I will not cut your hair." Lawrence went to another shop. The same thing happened.

Sometime later he was walking on Bethel's campus when Professor R. C. Kauffman was suddenly walking alongside him. "If you need a haircut, Lawrence, come over to my house and I will cut your hair," the professor told him. Lawrence did. Later, Lawrence found "a Holdeman barber, an ex-Marine in downtown Newton who asked no questions, simply cut my hair" (Hart, Interview Sept. 6, 2005). When Lawrence returned from military service to graduate from Bethel in 1961, he advocated strongly against racism, arguing that he had felt its dehumanizing effects.

Deep friendship with a hallmate, a classmate from Windom, Kansas, named Larry Kaufman, provoked the strongest questions for Lawrence with regard to the pacifist position. The two young men were in a church history course together and spent many hours discussing their faith and their plans.

With Larry Kaufman, Lawrence discussed the Mennonite peace tradition, or perhaps it became real to him in the way that he saw it lived out. The two college men spoke often to one another about their dreams. Lawrence wanted to go into the military to become a pilot, and Larry Kaufman was set on becoming part of the first group of PAX men to the Congo. The PAX program, taking its name from Latin for "peace," was a Mennonite Central Committee overseas program for conscientious objectors to military service. Larry knew Lawrence was planning to enlist in a navy aviation program for men with two years of college and that the plan was Lawrence's dream, but Larry never "shut him off" as Lawrence describes it today, even though they had chosen opposite paths of service.

When Lawrence shared the details of his friendship with Kaufman, it was with deep respect for Kaufman's effect on his life. What he seemed to admire most was the mutual respect, the long talks in which two young men could honestly share their dreams and respect their differences—a smalltown Kansas Mennonite youth's respect for the ideas and dreams of a smalltown Oklahoma Cheyenne Mennonite youth's dream to fly above the red earth he had been confined to. I was fascinated by the fact that they shared the name "Lawrence/Larry." In some ways they were two sides of the same coin at Bethel College.

Larry Kaufman drowned in the Congo's Kasai River on June 20, 1956, after fourteen months of voluntary service (Pauls 2004, 81). Learning of Larry's death, Lawrence was powerfully affected by what he knew of Larry's life choices and the way he had died. As Lawrence spoke about how he was struck by Larry's death, it seemed he somehow believed he had stayed alive for both of them. Although he was called out of the military by the designation of Peace Chief his grandfather had requested for him, he was strengthened in that decision by the dreams of peacemaker Larry, who lost his life in the Congo while serving as a PAX man. In Lawrence's words, "I came to think that if I was to lose my life, I wanted to lose it as Larry had, in the cause of peace" (June 17, 2003). It dawned on me, as Lawrence spoke of Larry's powerful influence on his own life choices—not only to leave the military but the many choices he has made since for living as a peacemaker—that Lawrence lives, to this day, for both of them. Lawrence is the peace chief and Mennonite minister who has absorbed both "Larrys'" dreams.

Lawrence minimized his career as a track athlete those first two years he spent at Bethel College, insisting that he was not really a star. Yet others remember his career there, and he remembers that track gave him some opportunities for interesting experiences. For example, he ran with a Bethel team at the KU Relays in Lawrence in an invitation for a small college sprint medley relay. While in Lawrence, Hart was sought out by the Haskell Indian Institute coach to meet with and encourage the Indian student athletes who were at the KU stadium. "He told them that they too could go to college and be on a track team. That was very gratifying. I still have the medal our team won" (E-mail correspondence, 2 September 2005).

After his two years (1951-53) at Bethel College as a track athlete, and after meeting Betty Bartel, who would become his life's partner,

Lawrence enlisted. He remembered that after extensive interviews, there were to be tests at Dallas Naval Air Station. His parents brought him to the Clinton airport, not far from where he lives today, to leave him in the little two-seater, single engine plane the Navy had sent to get Lawrence. There they gave him a helmet and put him into the cockpit. Then he headed for Dallas. It was Lawrence's first flight, and he was thrilled when he was given the control stick for a try. After two or three days of physical exams and tests, he was called back. He had survived. In October 1954 the next stop was Pensacola, Florida, for Basic Flight School. Upon completion of training that included landing on a carrier, he went to the Corpus Christi Advanced Training Command and was stationed at the Beeville Naval Auxiliary Air Station. In his sixteenth or seventeenth month, he became a commissioned officer; in his eighteenth month, he received his wings.

Lawrence remembers himself in his tailored uniform like Chester Tso and Bill Yazzie, those Navajo heroes of his youth that his grandfather had blessed with the eagle feather. He called his sister, Lucy, to ask her to come to be a part of his graduating ceremonies and asked her to pick up Betty on her way.

Almost fifty years after these heady times, I still sense the genuine excitement in Lawrence's eyes as he speaks of those flying days:

> We knew we were training pilots to become fighter pilots. I was in charge of young men. It was an adventure. As far as I know, I might have been the first "full-blood" pilot that summer of 1955 during those early years of jet aviation. In North Carolina, during fleet training, with a fighter squadron, all kinds of weather, flying the "soup" where vertigo was a problem, where you had to learn not to trust your senses, but trust your instruments—that was great stuff! I enjoyed that all-weather flying; I enjoyed landing on carriers. (June 17, 2003)

Lawrence remembered the vivid details of those times as he talked about the basic training he taught in Pensacola. He loved flying! He remembered difficult landings and still takes some pride in his abilities to hold his orientation in difficult circumstances. He recounted a time when he was the only one who knew the terrain, Okmulgee—on a night flight, when tested by the instructor. The others thought they were flying over Fort Smith! Lawrence knew the area.

Clearly, Lawrence had expected to make the military his career. He was good at it. He loved it. He was climbing the ranks. Then, in late 1957, in his third full year, assigned to a base in Texas, he realized that his grandfather was dying. Chief John P. Hart realized, too, that he did not have long. By January he was gone. But before he died, John P. Hart had gone to the other chiefs to request that they appoint Lawrence in his place. Normally, a chief does not pick his successor, Lawrence told me, nor does he necessarily pick someone in the family. However, the other chiefs agreed. Thus Lawrence was approached to become a principal chief, one of four principal chiefs among the traditional number of forty-four chiefs. Being so close emotionally to his grandfather, Lawrence said, he could not say no. He took it as a call.

But one cannot be a peace chief and continue to be a warrior. Perhaps it was at this point in our conversation that I saw again how destiny has worked in Lawrence's life. Consciously or unconsciously, Lawrence was becoming a warrior when he trained to become a fighter pilot. He was setting himself apart, cleansing his body, keeping pure from unhealthy influences like tobacco and alcohol, attending to his health and physique. The uniformed Navajo soldiers he had seen in his youth were the warrior-models he sought, the heroes he needed, bigger than life, blessed by the wisest man he knew, his grandfather. Lawrence agreed that it is fair to characterize these military years as his Dog Soldier days.

Now, however, especially in communication with his father, the Mennonite lay minister Homer Hart, who stayed in close contact with him during this decision, Lawrence agreed to become a chief. His family set June 15, 1958 as the date to set up the tepee and invite all the chiefs. They had to prepare all the food for the celebration, get the goods together needed for the giveaway (the traditional Cheyenne gift giving ceremony to honor those at an event), and get the two horses that would be given away. Lawrence would need to complete everything on that one day, June 15.

By this time, Lawrence was in his second tour of duty serving as a flight instructor in the Advanced Air Training Command in the Corpus Christi area. Several weeks before June 15, not anticipating that there should be a problem with taking this leave for such an important event, Lawrence went to his commanding officer to discuss his need for a leave. He hoped to drive home from South Texas to Hammon for the ceremonies.

Because it was near the end of the fiscal year and due to appropriations and budget issues, it turned out to be a most inopportune time for Lawrence to ask leave, and his commanding officer refused his request. At that time, at the end of the fiscal year, his commanding officer had to keep his planes in the air, anticipating fighter pilot needs in Saigon; they all had to keep working. His skipper tried to explain to Lawrence their need to spend down the money dispensed to them, to use their fuel so that they could expect a similar allocation in the upcoming year. What could Lawrence do but tell his folks that he could not return for this event of a lifetime they had been planning?

However, before Lawrence could make the call to his parents, the morning following the day of his request, his commanding officer sent for him. The summons surprised Lawrence. He had told no one of his disappointment about being unable to get leave to go back to Oklahoma for the defining event of his life.

"Lieutenant Hart," the commanding officer said, "I have been thinking about your ceremony. I think you need to go to that. We have filled out leave papers for you for a two-day leave. If you're back in two days, we'll tear them up. We'll give you a plane. You fly to Oklahoma. You can expend fuel there just as well; you can fly; you can train; go on to Oklahoma" (June 17, 2003).

Lawrence could hardly believe his ears. Because Sherman Base at Clinton was restricted, Lawrence chose to fly in to Altus Air Force Base. His family met him there.

Lawrence described the momentous day when he became a chief very simply: He met with the chiefs who gave him instructions in the tepee, they smoked, singers sang four songs, and the chiefs danced. Lawrence rode one of the two horses his parents had bought. The horses were given away. In other contexts he has recognized the great peace chiefs who gave him instructions: Chiefs Jacob Allrunner, Felix White Shield, John Heap of Birds, Henry Elk River, and Amos Hawk, among others (Hart, "Cheyenne Way of Peace and Justice" 2003, 262).

Stan Hoig, who has written about the Cheyenne peace chiefs, describes these traditional ceremonies and remarks upon the dignity and solemnity of such occasions as the chiefs smoking:

> When they had all seated themselves, the tribal priest brought
> forth his bag of kinnikinnick and opened it onto a cloth on the
> ground. He mixed the kinnikinnick well with herbs, bark, dried

leaves, and the marrow of buffalo bones. When the red-clay ceremonial pipe with its long stem, lavishly decorated with beads and
quills and feathers, was filled and lighted, the priest conducted a
long, solemn harangue to the sky spirit (*Heammawihio*, or the
Wise One Above), to the earth spirit (*Ahtunowhiho*, or the One
Who Lives Below the Ground), and to the wind spirits who
dwelled at the four points of the compass. The movement of the
pipe was in a crisscross fashion. (*Cheyenne Peace Chiefs* 1980, 6)

These ceremonies mark a momentous undertaking on the part of
the initiate. "A Cheyenne chief was required to be a man of peace, to be
brave, and to be of generous heart" (Hoig, *Cheyenne Peace Chiefs* 1980,
7). The stories are legend of the extraordinary efforts of the Cheyenne
peace chief's attempts at peacemaking and acts of bravery, but their profound acts of generosity were especially highlighted by the old historian
Grinnell who spoke of a way of being which finally shone from the peace
chief's very countenance:

> A good chief gave his whole heart and his whole mind to the work
> of helping his people, and strove for their welfare with an earnest-
> ness rarely equaled by the rulers of other men. Such thought for
> his fellows was not without its influence on the man himself; after
> a time the spirit of good-will which animated him became re-
> flected in his countenance, so that as he grew old such a chief
> often came to have a most benevolent and kindly expression.
> (quoted in Hoig, *Cheyenne Peace Chiefs* 1980, 11)

Indeed, Hoig argued that when the first settlers came to the Plains,
the Cheyennes were recognized above other tribes for their high culture,
their clean, chaste living, and their personal dignity. Furthermore, Hoig
believes they were also set apart from other tribes by their chieftain system which "demanded Christlike virtues from the men who led the tribe
and that produced strong, patient men of calm wisdom and good heart"
(Hoig, *Cheyenne Peace Chiefs* 1980, 14).

The most dramatic part of the story of the day that Hart was initiated into this chieftain system was his response to the event. He told
about this adventure with relish. For him it was clearly a marker of his
conversion, a climax to his warrior days, a celebration and an exit experience from the flying he loved. The high he experienced that day involved no alcohol or peyote but instead flying his plane at a height to

break the sound barrier. Lawrence clearly loved the contrasting elements of his twenty-four-hour sojourn—from his traditional horseback ride to Mach 1 in the sky. His life fused itself that day—from the simplest Cheyenne traditional ceremony, riding the horse into a circle of his people—to his return (to exit) his warrior life.

> Afterwards, I was driven to Altus Air Force base and flew back on a night flight to my base in south Texas. My return, which would have taken me twelve hours by car, took only fifty-five minutes in my jet fighter plane. I had plenty of fuel left as I checked in over the base and I got permission to burn down fuel. Flying south of Corpus Christi, I flew over the Gulf of Mexico at an altitude of 44,000 feet. I was about to create a sonic boom and I did not want to do it over a populated area, especially at night. I rolled my single engine, single seat, Swept Wing F-9-F Cougar over and pulled the nose down to make a vertical dive. It did not take long to go through Mach 1, the speed of sound. (Hart, "Cheyenne Way of Peace and Justice" 2003, 262-263)

From horseback through Mach 1 that same day must have truly felt like propulsion into another life! Lawrence told me the story quietly, his eyes shining with joy and maybe a bit of twinkling orneriness. He is adventuresome. "That's what I did . . . to get the experience, from the ancient experience to going over the Gulf."

Lawrence does not make his flight a symbolic act, but I am tempted to. What was the symbolism of breaking the sound barrier? Saying goodbye to cavalier ways? A fling of boyish reckless abandonment before he took on his responsibilities? He noted that he arrived home in Texas to tell Betty about the day's experiences—to tell about the ceremonies but not about the sound barrier. It seemed to be something he did for himself, a last fling, his own proving of himself. It is a story he has told over the years, without deconstruction of the symbolism, simply as a life story the way Chief Hart tells stories—here it is, make of it what you will!

Four months after he was made a principal chief of the Cheyenne people, Lawrence was out of the service, a peace chief. As a kind of postscript he tells me that once he was discharged, he tried to fly some small planes. The little aircraft just had no appeal.

CHAPTER FIFTEEN

IN MINISTRY:
HOMER AND JENNIE HART

I have connections to three religions—our own Cheyenne traditional religion, the Native American Traditional Church of my grandfather, my father's conversion to the Mennonite faith at age seventeen.
—Hart, Interview November 12, 2002

When Lawrence returned to Bethel College in 1960-1961 to finish his senior year, he was recently retired from four years in the military (1954-1958), married to Betty and with young child Connie, and a newly inducted chief to the Cheyenne people at his grandfather's request. He was also preparing for the ministry, following now in his own father's footsteps. Homer Hart was a lay minister for forty years in the Hammon Mennonite Church.

Lawrence loves to tell the stories of being a young boy in the pews during those years when Homer Hart became a very skilled interpreter for the Mennonite missionaries who delivered the sermons. Lawrence especially remembers his father interpreting for J. B. Ediger. Initially, Ediger would speak from his text a sentence or two; then Lawrence's father, Homer Hart would interpret, translating the text to Cheyenne. Lawrence says that he and Sam took great delight in listening to how their father interpreted, since they knew both languages. By Lawrence's senior year in high school, his father had become so skilled at his job that

Ediger would deliver his twenty-five-minute sermon and sit down—then Homer Hart would step up and interpret the entire sermon! Lawrence and Sam loved to sit in the pews and test their father. For example, if Ediger included a certain anecdote in his sermon, they waited to see if their father would remember to insert the story into his Cheyenne interpretation. Lawrence remembers with pride that his father would deliver an entire sermon in Cheyenne, not omitting the small anecdotes he and Sam were listening to hear!

Lawrence and his father grew closer after he lost his grandfather and as his father worked with him while Lawrence was away in the military, making the preparations for Lawrence to become one of the four principal chiefs of the Cheyennes. And now Lawrence began to look to Homer Hart as a model. Homer was a good preacher. Over the years he took on more and more responsibility as the missionaries left. Even in the early years, he often conducted funerals and preached sermons when the missionaries could not—acting entirely as a lay minister. He and Jennie were important models of church leadership for Lawrence.

Lawrence laughed when he pointed me to the account of his parents' courtship as recorded by Ruth Linscheid, who clearly took great joy in telling the story of the engagement of Homer Hart and Jennie Howling Water. Early one morning "big jolly Howling Water rode to the mission on his invariably too small pony, in an unusually excited manner. He reported that his beautiful daughter, Jenny, had been stolen in the night" (Linscheid, *Red Moon* 1973, 162). Homer had apparently practiced the Cheyenne tradition of a suitor coming to take his love to his own tepee—which Missionary Kliewer discouraged as "stealing a bride"—complete with dropping his hat near the Howling Water home. Jennie's father apparently pretended he did not know who her lover was. Linscheid's report actually sounded as if Chief Howling Water had simply come to the Kliewer home to proudly announce his daughter as fiancée to Kliewer's protégé, Homer Hart. Lawrence reminded me that Homer and Jennie did come to the mission and request a Christian wedding, which happened in May 1916.

Linscheid described Jennie Hart as beautiful, smart, and quick. She took organ lessons and practiced at the church; she also commented on Jennie's "neat sewing and beautiful bead work" (163) and neat and conveniently furnished farm home. Shortly after their marriage, Homer Hart transferred his membership to the Red Moon Mission Church and in 1917 became a paid worker of the mission. Linscheid referred to Homer Hart's "hopeful outlook" as well as his "stalwart faith." She added, "His uplifting spiritual influence was felt even by the white people of his community" (165).

Though Homer Hart was finally ordained as an elder of the Red Moon Mission Church in 1957, Linscheid says he chose to leave the full responsibilities to the missionary in residence. I asked Lawrence whether his father wanted more leadership. I was really wondering whether he chafed under this support role to the missionaries for forty years. Lawrence thought that his father might have liked more training. As a lay leader, however, Lawrence said that his gifts were adequate. Lawrence remembered that Ediger came to do services at the church twice a month. If he was not available, Homer Hart did the services.

I once asked Lawrence to compare the personalities and gifts of his father and grandfather. Lawrence said,

> I don't think about the contrasts they may have had. They both worked very hard on the small farm they had. My grandfather had a few horses. I helped my grandfather harness them and go six miles to town, generally on a Saturday, to be there by noon, spend the afternoon, come home again. He did lots of farming while he was able. Then my father took over the operation. My father got him a tractor and combine, and we'd have a good crop of wheat which he cut before he cut for other families. I would go with him to help harvest, and ride in the wheat bin!
>
> I don't know what the farmers thought when they broke for lunch and here I crawled out of the wheat bin and sat down before a plate! I always got to eat with them. I watched him work hard during the week; he devoted weekends to the church. My father helped with visitations and funerals. Sometimes he worked directly with the funeral directors themselves—Leo Schneider, Vernon Kiesau, and Elgin Kern. He was very good friends with them. They would depend completely on him in Hammon, not on Rev. Ediger or later, Rev. Friesen. . . . What was important to my father were his peers, the other native lay leaders in Clinton, Thomas, Weatherford, Deer Creek, Seiling, Canton, people like Guy Heap of Birds or John Heap of Birds, Willie Meeks. There were several others. These men would get together and meet with

the missionaries, study together, get their informal training, study Scriptures together. It was a kind of informal seminary for him and his Cheyenne and Arapaho peers. My father enjoyed these times, the leadership training. He wasn't alone. (Hart, Interview March 4, 2004)

Though he was unwilling to contrast his father with his paternal grandfather, Lawrence willingly talked about a trait he felt was strongly instilled in him by both men—the virtue of self-sufficiency. He recalled that while a small boy he helped both his grandfather and father with combine work. His job was to reach up into the machine and clear out the compacted straw which clogged the machine. He rode in the bin until the straw needed to be cleared. Then his dad opened a small door through which Lawrence extended a small hand and cleared out the straw. He considered his task small but important. They relied on him to do the job.

The trait of self-reliance has been an important value for Lawrence. For evidence, he pointed to his own education. Through all of his college and seminary years, he did not receive financial assistance from the Cheyenne and Arapaho tribes.

I personally know how hard it is to finance higher education. That is why I insisted that a scholarship trust be created, using the accumulated interest of the fifteen million dollar settlement by the U. S. Court of Claims [owed the Cheyenne tribes]. A Scholarship Trust Fund established by the fifteenth Business Committee has helped to educate many, many Cheyenne and Arapaho students over the years. (Hart E-mail, October 4, 2005).

Lawrence has continued that practice of self-reliance as he and Betty maintain the Cheyenne Cultural Center, which has never been supported by Tribal funds.

I wondered if Lawrence's father Homer had encouraged him to go into the ministry. Lawrence answered, "He let me decide." But Lawrence continued,

I think he was grateful to Rev. Arthur Friesen who counseled us. It was probably my dad who set up these counseling appointments or perhaps asked Arthur Friesen to come talk to us. We'd help with Vacation Bible School, help with meeting other Christian leaders. We went to Bethel. He came up as often as he could to see us at Bethel. When I ran in track, he came to Bethel to watch me run. . . . Maybe he made me run harder. [Lawrence smiles.] (March 4, 2004)

Lawrence tried to remember whether his father witnessed his early years of pastoring. He remembered that his father came to his wedding to Betty at the Bruderthal Mennonite Church near Hillsboro. He believed his father was still around when he was ordained.

"What would your father and grandfather say about this Cheyenne Cultural Center," I wondered aloud, looking around at the site of the interview.

I think they would see it as something of value when no one has time to listen to a father or grandfather's stories. If you want to know such information, this is a poor substitute, but one can become absorbed in one's culture here, one's language. In their days, [storytelling] was the entertainment. While we helped them in their tasks, we listened to what they had to say. (March 4, 2004)

Lawrence referred then to the traditional "shades" or brush arbors Cheyenne families loved to sit under together—out of the sun—to talk. When the missionaries came to Oklahoma, they worshipped under these Cheyenne family arbors, common then to most Cheyenne families. These brush arbors are good symbols, Lawrence says, of the Cheyenne interest in family life.

Then something about that memory of family life under the old brush arbor set Lawrence to thinking about Cheyenne ways of discipline. Especially, he remembered his own father.

The thing about my father, rearing Sam and me—and we weren't model kids!—one thing that I really have marveled at about him, in his discipline, is that he never touched us. No spanking, no whipping, just talking. . . . That is so unbelievable. In the kind of discipline he had, which he must have learned from my grandfather, it worked. Surely, there must have been some punishment, but nothing like a "hit." I know when we would sit in the pews, Ediger would come sit with us, as if we were going to misbehave! (March 4, 2004)

I commented that perhaps their father loved them into behaving well. I have read that traditional Cheyenne discipline was about "being with" children. Lawrence nodded and reflected.

> I remember many times when Dad would take us fishing to be with us. To bring home some fish for dinner. We would often do that. Later on, during the spring, at the Howling Water place, the allotment just north of the church a mile east, on Sundays we would hunt soft shelled turtles. My father could spot their long snouts sticking out of the sand. We'd make soup. My mother would boil them. Sometimes [my dad] would bait and catch snapping turtles. We would bake the snapping turtles. Wash them. Gut them. Clean them out good. Then, bake them in the shell. Maybe cover them like you would a turkey. Those were meaningful Sunday afternoons at the Howling Water place. In fall, my father would begin to chop wood. We would get a stack of wood for heat and for my mother's cook stove.

Lawrence clearly honors these times of "just being with" his father. I saw then that at least one of the functions of the Cheyenne Cultural Center is a place for children to "be with" their elders.

When I inquired about Lawrence's relationships with his siblings, he remarked that the only ones in his family that he really got to know during his childhood were his older brother Sam and his younger sister Ramona, the youngest child of the family. His older siblings went to boarding schools.

Arthur Friesen and his wife Viola were the last Mennonite missionary couple to minister to the Hammon church where Homer and Jennie Hart served so many years. They worked closely with the Harts at Hammon for ten years and remembered his parents when they introduced Lawrence as a special speaker for the Mission Festival at the First Mennonite Church in Reedley, California, in October 1981. They referred to Jennie Hart as "one of the finest Christian women" they had known, citing Proverbs 31:23-29 as a description of her. After references to strength, dignity, and the teaching of kindness, that Scripture passage ends with these words: "Her children rise up and call her happy; her husband too, and he praises her: Many women have done excellently, but you surpass them all."

Addressing Lawrence, they said about his father,

Isaiah describes a messenger of peace, "How beautiful upon the mountains are the feet of him who brings good tidings, who publishes peace, who brings good tidings of good, who publishes salvation, who says to Zion, 'Your God reigns.'" Your father did that for forty years. . . . It was your parents' hope and prayer that one of their children would follow in their footsteps. May God give you strength and wisdom as you endeavor to do this. (Friesen, 1981, n.p.)

CHAPTER SIXTEEN

CROSSING OVER; COMING BACK

The story goes, according to his Mennonite pastor, that while still a high school youth, Lawrence went to visit Reverend Arthur Friesen. He sat down in his pastor's study to talk about going to college, to get the pastor's recommendations. Well, he told Lawrence, there's Bacone Indian College in eastern Oklahoma which I believe to be a fine school; then there's my own alma mater, Bethel College, which is an excellent college. Rev. Friesen remembers that Lawrence remarked that day in his study that since he would have to live with white people, he might as well start now. He would go to Bethel College. Rev. Friesen was immensely pleased.
—Arthur and Viola Friesen, "Introduction" 1981, 2

When Lawrence went to Bethel for his first two years, 1953-55, it was primarily to get the two years of college he needed to get into the military and fulfill his dream of becoming a fighter pilot. He ran track, apparently intent on staying in good physical shape, to retain the physical prowess he had imagined he must achieve to reach his military goals. However, he also developed some crucial friendships that shaped his life from that earliest stint at Bethel College. Larry Kaufman, his good friend who drowned in the Congo while serving in PAX, had an important impact on Lawrence's life choices. Most importantly, however, he met Betty Bartel, a young Mennonite woman of German ancestry from Hillsboro, Kansas, who was to become his life's partner.

When I first saw Betty, dressed in traditional Cheyenne garb as the family reenacted a Cheyenne ceremonial dance that included her husband and children, I assumed that she was a Cheyenne. But Betty was not born Cheyenne.

Betty Bartel and Lawrence Hart were sophomores at Bethel College, and both had been chosen to serve for the Junior-Senior Banquet. Since the theme was centered around a reenactment of King Arthur's Court, they both had to wear the gunny sack garb of court servants. Unfortunately (or rather, as it turned out, fortunately), Lawrence had on his good black shoes, and as Betty went by him carrying a bowl of "gloppy peas," as she recalled, she spilled them on Lawrence's shoes!

Betty thought she had adequately cleaned up her mess, but her good friend, a classmate from Puerto Rico, told Betty that she owed Lawrence an apology; those were obviously good shoes and probably brand new! Furthermore, she convinced Betty that Lawrence probably did not even have any black shoe polish to fix the mess Betty had created. Betty duly apologized, and offered to Lawrence that she would clean his shoes. She seemed surprised to acknowledge to me that he gave them to her. He probably knew that this would give him an excuse to come get them.

Betty cleaned, polished, even buffed the shoes. And after Lawrence came to pick them up, they began to talk, and eventually to date.

When I asked Betty if it mattered in the 1950s that she was dating a young man who was a Cheyenne, Betty said, "Well, I didn't really notice" (June 17, 2003). Furthermore, they did not really consider themselves dating. Her Puerto Rican friend and her fiancée plus Betty and Lawrence would go to Betty's folks for a good meal. In fact, Betty thinks eventually the more sensitive issue in their courtship for her was Lawrence's interest in the military rather than that he was Cheyenne. Her home church near Hillsboro, Kansas, the Bruderthal Mennonite Church, did not look favorably on military service among Mennonite youth. In fact, Betty remembers that initially she was shocked when Lawrence told her of his plans. She has a vague memory of saying, "Are you sure you want to go into the military?" Years later, when Lawrence and Betty moved back to Oklahoma as a young ministerial couple, she noted that her real culture shock was not so much in becoming a part of the Cheyenne community but that the other pastors in the area did not seem to have the strong peace orientation she had been raised to believe in as a Bruderthal youth.

Lawrence and Betty corresponded during his years in the military service. They also tried to talk by phone on a party line on which everyone was listening. Finally, they had to work out a system whereby Lawrence called to signal her, then Betty drove into town to her grandparents' house because they had a private line where he would call her back, and they could then have some privacy.

Actually, Betty first went home with Lawrence to meet his family in Oklahoma the July following their sophomore year. Betty remembered especially the service at the little country church, Hammon Mennonite, Lawrence's home church. After the service, all the attenders spread blankets under the trees, took out the food they had packed, and shared with any guests present. Betty remembered Lawrence's mother, Jennie Hart, spreading her blanket and sitting as all her family ate her fried chicken.

How did they dress, I asked? Just good cotton simple clothes, Betty remembered. She also remembered that her wise Puerto Rican friend prepared her to go visit Lawrence's family. "Don't go there wearing shorts," Betty's friend admonished her. Betty wore pedal pushers.

Lawrence and Betty were married after Betty finished college, although they could not marry on the date originally planned because Lawrence was on a mission out of Beeville, Texas, where he was then stationed. After they married, Betty joined him at Beeville and taught school at Woodsboro, Texas.

Betty and Lawrence did have some difficulty with the wedding itself. Betty's pastor at Bruderthal did not want to marry them because Lawrence was in the military. Lawrence said they did not want him to wear his uniform at the wedding service. He had no objection as he had not intended to wear the uniform. Betty desperately wanted to be married at Bruderthal, her home church, in a community she treasured. Thus she asked John Thiessen, a longtime missionary and pastor friend in North Newton, to marry them at Bruderthal, and the church fathers finally agreed. "That was my church community," Betty remembered, "and I was determined that I would be married in my own church— even if the pastor felt that he could not marry us." Betty also remembered that many years later, perhaps at Betty's mother's funeral, the chair of the deacons apologized for the church's behavior in this incident. It had bothered him for many years.

When they came back to Oklahoma, their first child Connie was a baby. Since Lawrence's mother was not well, they tried to stay close and help. She died after having gall bladder surgery. Betty said that she was a "bleeder" and bled to death after the surgery. Connie, Lawrence, and Betty lived in the little house on the Hart home place. Lawrence knew he needed to finish college but decided to stay near after his mother's death, and he attended Southwestern University at Weatherford for a year. Then they moved to a rental home in Corn, where Betty taught third grade. There they involved themselves with the Bergthal Church, the General Conference Mennonite church just outside Corn.

During the summers they helped on the Val and Wayne Krehbiel farms near Hydro (Hart, Interview March 22, 2005). Wayne and his wife Fern were custom harvesters and left their farm in the charge of Lawrence and Betty while they followed the harvest from south of the Red River to the Dakotas. Lawrence and Betty lived in their house while Lawrence worked their land and Betty managed their garden and learned how to milk their cow. Lawrence truly enjoyed their lifestyle on the Krehbiel farms. He loved driving the D2 Caterpillar tractor over their many acres, trying to keep the sandy soil from blowing. Wherever he could, Lawrence helped as an intern pastor with services at local churches, sometimes at the Bergthal Church or assisting Paul Isaak at Bethel Mennonite.

Then they moved on to Bethel for Lawrence to finish his undergraduate work. Lawrence said that he thought he had done good academic work during his three semesters at Southwestern, making the Dean's Honor Roll for two semesters and the President's Honor Roll one semester. However, he felt that doing his senior year at Bethel toughened him academically as he prepared to go on to Associated Mennonite Biblical Seminary (AMBS) in Elkhart, Indiana. Lawrence chuckled to remember that at Bethel the competition was keen; he was "just another student," as he remembered it, and had to work hard for his grades (March 22, 2005).

At Bethel the second time, he continued his "ministry inquiry" experiences and preparations to go to AMBS. He laughed as he recalled that he and Monte Fey, a classmate preparing to become a Presbyterian minister, suffered through Greek class—always outdone by a certain Lois Heidebrecht who raised the curve too high. They could never figure out what reason she could have for needing a Greek class! Fey worked for

Century Clothing, the men's store in downtown Newton, and he offered to help Lawrence find a "pulpit suit" there. Lawrence continued to work Sundays where he could. He remembered especially Pastor Paul Goering at the Lorraine Avenue Church in Wichita, a graduate of Yale Divinity School, who mentored Lawrence and would later preach at his ordination in Oklahoma. Meanwhile Betty supported their family with her teaching job at Walton. Betty remembered fondly her daughter Connie being in an experimental learning class at Bethel with children's literature professor Blanche Spaulding. Mrs. Spaulding encouraged her to read to her children, to find the best books of all cultures, including Cheyenne.

There is good evidence of Lawrence's seriousness about ministry and vocation when he returned to Bethel to graduate in 1961. The 1961 yearbook pictured him as one of seven in the Church Worker's Fellowship, an organization described as being "open to anyone planning to enter some phase of full-time Christian service." In addition, he became political. A good example was a spring controversy on campus in 1961 and the way Lawrence weighed in on the issue.

The Bethel Peace Club had gone to Nashville for a human rights conference, and an African student had been refused service because of his color when he tried to check in to the Allen Hotel with the others. Someone in the Peace Club group had gone with the African student to stay elsewhere, but the debate on campus afterward centered on whether any of the Bethel delegation should have stayed at the Allen Hotel given its discriminatory policy.

The Bethel Collegian, the college's newspaper, posed an editorial question, "What do you consider the crucial issues involved in the Nashville Hotel incident?" Lawrence's letter declared his separation from the Bethel delegation and its representation of the Bethel student body. He perceived that the group did not take a stand against the discrimination. He declared his own solidarity with the one who had suffered discrimination. "The deep hurt which ensued upon one individual prompts this voice of separation, for I know personally the abasement one suffers in racial discrimination. To have it approved by peers is more painful." He declared his separation from those in the delegation whom he saw as indifferent: "I refuse to be a part of the educated deception and indifference characterized by some of our delegates. Through this medium I hereby disavow my being represented by the recent study delegation to Nashville, Tennessee" (*Bethel Collegian*, March 30, 1961).

The social science seminar paper that Lawrence wrote for his final project for graduation at Bethel College was titled, "Why the Doctrine of Nonresistance Has Failed to Appeal to the Cheyenne Indian." In the preface he documented his own "conversion experience":

> I once held in my hands the capabilities of leveling and destroy-
> ing a target larger than the area covering the city of Newton. Now
> with the same hands I am within reach of ministering to a large
> segment of a defined population. On the one hand, as a typical
> Cheyenne Warrior, I have been extremely proud of my prowess.
> On the other, I have had a realization that the targets to which I
> had been assigned are and were not entirely non-material, and
> that destroying everything within those targets or anywhere else
> is not the ultimate answer. (Hart, 1961, n.p.)

Lawrence stood, at this point in his career, both inside and outside the Cheyenne community, as he sought to look at the issue of nonresistance as it concerned the Cheyenne community. He challenged his own people and his own history: "As Head Chief of the Southern Cheyenne, I direct this question to my people, 'How soon shall we, if ever, reach the point of pacifism we once practiced long before the coming of the "spiders" [whites or non-Cheyennes]?'" His social science seminar paper included brief histories of the Cheyenne people and the Mennonite mission work to the Southern Cheyennes. With regard to the question of nonresistance, he argued that the Cheyennes need to know about their own historical peace tradition and should also be made more aware of Mennonite theology with regard to pacifism. He argued for shoring up the efforts of Mennonite missionaries in Oklahoma with materials and emotional support.

He asked for protests against the television industry's stereotype of the Indian: "The Indian has forgiven the white man; it is now time that the white man forgive the Indian" (23). He argued for teaching the Cheyennes their native tongue and noted the Mennonite historical concern to preserve the Cheyenne language (23-24). He pressed for teaching his people nonresistance: "Let us therefore present this doctrine to the Cheyenne. . . . If a Cheyenne is humiliated by the general public for a peace stand, the humiliation will not be a new experience" (1961, 24).

The paper read like a manifesto and a specific course of action, ending with proposals. He was headed for the Associated Mennonite Biblical Seminary in Elkhart, Indiana, where he studied for two years before he returned to Oklahoma and the Koinonia Church to work on his agenda.

The summer after he graduated, Lawrence and Betty often went to Hillsboro to stay with Betty's parents and to work for her uncle or her Grandfather Funk. Lawrence highly respected the work ethic of Betty's Grandpa Funk. He was up early and in the fields when Lawrence arrived. They took a fifteen-minute break promptly at 9:00 a.m. for rolls and coffee. At noon, Grandpa Funk took a short nap. At 3:00 p.m., again the fifteen-minute break. He worked hard, and, as Lawrence noted, though quite well off, he lived simply, and Grandpa Funk was able to pay Lawrence for his help that summer. Other "pay" they received that summer included a hog which was butchered, smoked, frozen, and prepared so that they could take the meat with them to AMBS.

However, when the time came to leave that fall, their second child, Nathan, was born in Marion, Kansas. With the help of a brother-in-law, Lawrence went ahead with their moving van. Betty waited a month until Lawrence could return for her and the children.

When I asked Lawrence about his AMBS experience, he pointed to key professors, such as Howard Charles, who impressed him. He remembered learning that the joint programs between Goshen and Elkhart (the old Chicago seminary) meant the more conservative Mennonite dress of coat and collar for certain professors at Goshen, and the coat and tie at Elkhart! He learned to recognize and respect important Mennonite leaders like Harold Bender for his recovery of the Anabaptist vision. He especially recalled with fondness his professors who taught preaching: Roy Umble, Paul Miller, and Erland Waltner. He enrolled in a B.D. program rather than the M.R.E. degree program, which he later regretted, but he acknowledged that the family was running out of funds, despite their best efforts. Betty and another seminary wife shared teaching jobs babysitting children, and Lawrence did whatever moonlighting he could, working at one point for the Elkhart school system, preparing students for the GED.

After two years at the Seminary, Lawrence and Betty received the call to come serve the Koinonia Mennonite Church congregation east of

Clinton, Oklahoma. The missionaries had left, and the congregation was searching for a pastor. In September 1963, Lawrence and Betty were commissioned before their home congregation in Hammon by pastor Ralph Weber.

Lawrence and Betty moved into the old parsonage alongside the old barn on the twenty-acre site of the old mission station. The church had been moved off the site by that time, and the mission board expected them to sell the place. They tried. Lots of people came to look at it. As Lawrence recalled it, the more they polished their real estate pitch, the more they talked themselves into buying it! The place needed work. It had an old cistern for water. There was no sewage system. The electrical system was decrepit. But they bought it, and Lawrence said it was the best thing they ever did. They made themselves a home, worked from a central site, and settled in to pastor the Koinonia Church for the next forty years, assisting the other local churches. There were still missionaries at Hammon, Canton, and Seiling when they returned to Oklahoma. They would get together once a month, all of them taking turns at the Sunday ministries at the Concho Indian School.

It must have been a tightrope to walk for Lawrence and Betty when they returned to Oklahoma to pastor. They were not traditional Anglo Mennonite missionaries. They were not native helpers working with missionaries as Lawrence's parents had been. They were seminary-trained pastors responsible for right theology. And they came back during the 1960s, when times were changing everywhere in American culture and American churches.

When I try to imagine those early times for Lawrence and Betty in Oklahoma pastoring the Koinonia Church at Clinton, I am struck by how often the women in a community work in each human social circle at integrating newcomers. This seemed true for Lawrence and Betty as they came back to pastor the church. I asked Betty how she needed help and wisdom to become part of the Cheyenne community and church. She pointed to the women of the church as the leaders when they returned to Oklahoma. She remembered that soon after they returned, they were attending a memorial service for a church leader, a chief. When the chiefs were asked to dance, Lawrence sat—until the women came and told him he should dance. When I asked about the use of Cheyenne language in the church, Betty noted that early on Lawrence called on the older women to pray in Cheyenne in church. Then she remembered slow incorporation of Cheyenne elements, fry bread at communion, for example. The men the missionaries had trained were mostly gone. The women were there.

She spoke with special admiration for the Star Mission Club. On Mondays the women of the church would gather for potluck and quilting. When Betty arrived, announcing to the group that she was not sure what their expectations were for her as pastor's wife, Alice Heap of Birds, a notable leader in the church, assured Betty that they had been well-trained by the missionaries who had gone before; they knew what to do in their Star Mission Club! They wondered, would Betty be willing to wash the tea towels? Betty laughed at the memory. She came, a young, experienced professional in education, and was assigned to wash the tea towels! She admitted that she did have a washing machine, and not all of the women did.

Betty came to respect deeply the women of the Star Mission Club for their genuine faith and spiritual care of one another. The women talked of those in their community who were ill, those who needed help. Openly and honestly they expressed their own needs. Betty had been taught by her German Mennonite community that one does not publicly share one's difficulties. These Cheyenne women honestly and sincerely shared their pains and sorrows in prayer. And they took care of the community together.

I sense that Betty, placed in the role of the traditional missionary wife both by tradition and the expectations of other Oklahoma pastors, sometimes felt stifled. She wanted to use the profession for which she had trained. She was an educated professional, and she was not always allowed to use those gifts. She took in some twenty-one foster children during those years. Then she worked with the local children's shelter.

Both Lawrence and Betty worked with a committee of concern to address issues of alcohol use in the community. In fact, their work with alcohol abuse began, Lawrence said,

> when Betty, Connie, and Nathan consented to use our vacation money to go to study at the Center for Alcohol Studies at Rutgers University. I was likely the first tribal leader to recognize the problem of alcoholism among our Indian population state and nationwide. Much came from that beginning in 1969, including the first effort in the nation to address alcoholism among Indian people. (E-mail correspondence, 2 September 2005)

Lawrence and Betty were founders of a youth shelter in Clinton that has become Multi-County Youth Services. They worked to develop leadership in mission churches in Seiling, Canton, Hammon, and Clinton. Betty also worked like her mother-in-law before her to teach at the church, play organ, tell stories, provide meals—to teach, minister, and administer (Heinrichs 1985, 13-14).

When Lawrence came back to Oklahoma to serve the church and the tribe, he quickly became involved in tribal leadership as a spokesman and negotiator. When I asked him to recount some of the work in which he was involved that made a difference, he pointed to the role he served as chairman of the tribes for the fifteenth Business Committee in 1969. The role in those years was pretty much uncompensated except for allowances for phone calls and official trips. However, the role was very demanding (Hart, Interview Oct. 20, 2004). Lawrence clearly threw himself into his role as chairman and was able to accomplish a huge amount of work in those two years.

When Congress established the Special Claims Commission, it was determined that the tribe had not been compensated fair market value for lands bought from them, and that they were owed a huge amount of money. The figure after compromise was 15 million dollars for the Cheyenne tribe. Obviously, various persons among the tribe wanted to program this money in different ways. Lawrence learned quickly that the people who would benefit, now scattered across the country, really wanted a per capita distribution. The Committee's role was to urge the government to distribute the money in this way, to enact special legislation to get this done.

Lawrence remembered that others believed that the Business Committee did not have a chance to make this distribution happen. However, the fifteenth Business Committee, seven others along with Lawrence as chair, got busy. They hired an attorney who drafted the bill for them. As chair of the group, Lawrence traveled around the country, taking the testimony of the people from Los Angeles to Denver to Albuquerque, trying to discern the will of the people (Oct. 20, 2004).

Then they appeared before Congress. This was Lawrence's first time to testify, and he chuckled softly, remembering how the Committee strategized.

We wanted to impress the subcommittee with how educated and sophisticated we were. We supposed such a tactic would win the day. I was a college graduate, had two years of seminary. Henrietta White Man, I believe, had her master's degree. We men put on our business suits, as did the women. Then we watched as we were followed in our testimony by Vine Deloria Jr, who had brought from El Paso Tewa people dressed in native clothing and using an interpreter. They made a bigger impression than we did. They didn't get many questions, and a Do Pass. We were grilled! (Oct. 20, 2004)

But the fifteenth Business Committee also was successful in its request, probably because its members had thoughtfully made plans to have the children's shares (for those under eighteen) of the money put into trusts in Oklahoma banks until they reached maturity. They had also set aside a half-million dollars in a scholarship fund for post-high school students. Both of these projects appealed to the subcommittee of Congress.

In his statement before the Indian Affairs Subcommittee of the Senate Committee on Interior and Insular Affairs in August 1967 on S. 1933, Hart argued in defense of the per capita distribution and for the right of the Cheyenne Arapaho people to determine their own destiny. "There is a vast difference between a plan designed by the people and a program designed for the people. . . . We are aware that programs have been designed for us. Too often we have had to adjust and change to fit into a preconceived mold. Why not let us design a plan to meet our problems and needs?" (Hart 1967, 6). He spoke for his tribe: "The outright per capita payment of the judgment fund to the self-supporting and self-sustaining adult members of our tribes will mean that at long last they are recognized as mature, intelligent people" (6). The Business Committee was heard, and the people's wishes were granted.

Another way in which Chief Hart served his tribe was in securing lands declared surplus by the U.S. government. Because he was aware of this governmental declaration of surplus land it could no longer use, he was able to procure for the tribe the ninety acres adjacent to the allotment on which the Cheyenne Cultural Center stands today. Important programs and resources were built on that land. First, the Community Center and Hall was established, followed by the Elderly Nutrition Center, an Emergency Medical Unit with two ambulances and their own EMT, an office for a social worker, and a child development center. The casino the tribe built there is now five years old and there is a Head

Start center and a drug treatment center. Lawrence said, after listing these services now available, "I had always hoped for a facility, living arrangements for the elderly. The tribe isn't going to do that, but the Housing Authority is going to do that just outside the boundaries of that land" (Oct. 20, 2004).

When I asked about the work of the Housing Authority in Hammon, which I knew Lawrence had helped to establish, he acknowledged that one of the last things he did while he was chair was to sign documents to establish the Housing Authority in 1970. Later, the next Business Committee organized the Housing Authority which grants monies and awards new housing to applicants.

In the course of my interviews with Lawrence, he returned again and again to recognize the work accomplished by the fifteenth Business Committee which he chaired. For example, he was invited during that time as a tribal leader to a conference in Denver to determine if a new federal Indian education agency should be established to work on findings of the Robert Kennedy Report on Indian Education. He remembered arguing, along with Vine Deloria Jr. and Phillip Martin, chairman of the Mississippi Choctaws, that the Indian Education Office not be lodged in the Interior Department, Bureau of Indian Affairs but rather in the new Office of Education. The Office of Education became a department and that is where the Indian Education Office is lodged today (E-mail Correspondence, 2 September 2005).

The Cheyenne Cultural Center is a four-acre complex just east of Clinton on Route 66. Very visible and clearly marked, it is nestled so naturally into its surroundings that it seems as if it has always existed here. The buildings, however, feel relatively new given that the Center was incorporated on February 25, 1977. It is wonderfully accessible, as are both Lawrence and Betty Hart. Together, they run the Center as an art and history center, language learning lab, museum, interpretive center, and hosting site for many major events.

As one pulls off Route 66 to enter the complex, one notes immediately the marker at the entry gate, The Red Wheat Historical Marker. This marker allows the Cheyenne Cultural Center to introduce the historical connection which exists among the Cheyenne, Arapaho, and Mennonite peoples. The original Cheyenne and Arapaho Reservation was divided into 160-acre allotments, and the Jerome Commission was charged to record the allotments. Working under severe time constraints, staff at the Darlington School helped in the translation of Indian names. Most of the Cheyenne and Arapaho people were unable to speak English. Of course, the workers at Darlington were Mennonites, immigrants from Russia who had introduced turkey red wheat to the U.S. in the 1870s when they came (notes from Cheyenne Cultural Center handout, "The Red Wheat Historical Marker").

In a 1992 Quincentennial Address, Hart said of the Red Wheat marker, "The name 'Red Wheat' has become highly symbolic. It symbolizes the meeting of two cultures—through an act of God" (Hart 1992, 8). The Cheyenne Cultural Center Centennial handout tells the story of Red Wheat:

> The SW ¼ of Section 18, Township 12 North, Range 16 West, Indian Meridian, was selected by a Cheyenne woman as her allotment. Her name was translated as Red Wheat. After allotments were chosen, the remaining were opened for settlement in a Land Run held at noon, April 19, 1892. Red Wheat's Allotment was partitioned for a railroad and U.S. Highway 66, now the historic Route 66.

The birth date of Cheyenne woman Red Wheat is not recorded. Red Wheat generously deeded 20 acres of the SE ¼ of her Allotment #79 to the General Conference Mennonite Church Board of Missions. A church was built and dedicated in 1898 to serve Red Wheat's people. This year marks the centennial. The Original Allottee has many descendants. Red Wheat died on April 14, 1913 ("The Red Wheat Historical Marker").

When I asked Lawrence how the Cheyenne Cultural Center came to be, he described it as a kind of natural occurrence—I had an image of an elder's blessing which simply caused the Cultural Center to emerge as an outgrowth along Turtle Creek something like a mushroom! Apparently, some years after Lawrence and Betty came back to Oklahoma in 1963, Dr. Karl Schleiser, an anthropologist at Wichita State University, wanted to meet the Arrow Keeper. The contact came through Dr. James Juhnke, history professor at Bethel College. Obligingly, Chief Hart invited the anthropologist and the Arrow Keeper to meet along Turtle Creek. They sat together out in the open air because Lawrence did not then own a tepee. Betty prepared a traditional meal, Lawrence noted, as called for by protocol. They talked about creating a non-profit corporation, and in open discussions created Cheyenne and Arapaho Research and Development, an organization now defunct. In a separate conversation, the Arrow Keeper asked Lawrence to create a separate organization, and from this latter grew the Cheyenne Cultural Center. Lawrence wrote, "The Keeper came to the first event sponsored by CCC, The Four Directions Indian Art Festival. I found the Keeper to be intelligent with good knowledge. I have always felt that the success of CCC emanated from power he imparted. We were good friends" (E-mail correspondence, 2 September 2005).

I have spent many hours at the Cheyenne Cultural Center, visiting exhibits, touring with students and friends, listening to Lawrence's lectures, following tours with Betty among the artifacts, thumbing through books, watching dancers in the center pavilion, walking the grounds and checking the labeled plants. Of course, I have done most of my interviews of Lawrence and Betty there as well. Often, visitors stop and ask questions. The telephone rings frequently with someone's request for information. I remember the call which came from a television station wanting a clarification on how the Cheyenne language refers to The Big Dipper. Did they ever call it The Big Bear? Lawrence was puzzled. They dug through the Petter dictionary. They consulted with Lenora, Lawrence's sister, the linguist. Lenora said she would call Aunt Blanche who is the family encyclopedia of oral tradition. I noted with gratitude that the Cheyenne language has been preserved, and there is a "Center" where it is available—a key legacy of the Mennonites' work together with the Cheyenne people.

The consistent thread through the Harts' forty years of service in Oklahoma has been their ministry to the Koinonia Church. I have worshipped with them there in recent years. As I write, Koinonia suffers the same rural depopulation that many small rural Mennonite churches are experiencing. Betty noted that on Easter Sunday there may be fifty in attendance, but that on other Sundays, Lawrence may teach the Sunday school lesson to no more than ten people. Rather than a full-blown sermon, he often does a biblical interpretation.

On the Sunday in April when the Historical Committee of the Mennonite Church USA met with the Koinonia congregation, they put together a special bulletin and service for the visitors. The bulletin cover is a sketch captioned HAOENAOM, "The First Mission in This Community" with the following note:

Rev. M. M. Horsch was a Mennonite missionary who came among a band of Cheyenne in this community in 1896. Our ancestors worshipped under brush arbors until the building shown above was built. It was known as the Haoenaom Station, dedicated in 1898. The photograph was taken in 1906 three years after Clinton was founded. (Koinonia Mennonite Church Bulletin, April 18, 2004)

The building and the grounds show their age.

Worship service began with a prelude by Betty on the organ. Lawrence called us to worship. He sat on the side of the church and talked easily and informally from there, calling out a hymn change or an announcement. When he went to the front to assume the pastor's role, his voice took on a ceremonial depth, as it did when he led out in the singing of hymns, especially those in Cheyenne, sung from the Cheyenne hymnal. It seemed to me that I had only heard him in this voice previously when he prayed before going onto the Washita Site. I wondered whether it is a preaching voice he learned from his father.

Betty sat by Lawrence with her granddaughter and moved easily to the altar table to tell the wonderful children's story with native figures. Lawrence's sister, Lenora Hart, gave the invocation in Cheyenne. Scripture was read in English and Cheyenne. The offering was for local expenses. Lawrence preached on "The Way, Truth and Life."

Afterward, a traditional meal was served: three kinds of soup, rice with raisins (a traditional food because raisins and prunes were commodities given the Indians by the U.S. Government), a huge basket of fry bread, and various other dishes. All of the food was carried onto tables out of the tiny kitchen. We passed by, buffet-style, guests first.

When I attended at Koinonia again in spring 2005, we were worshiping alongside those who came for the first meeting of Native Mennonite Ministries. Willis Busenitz of the Montana Cheyenne Mennonite Church preached, and we had a communion service. God is building his kingdom among native peoples, Pastor Busenitz said. Speaking for the native Christians, he continued, "I am convinced that the Mennonite church needs us as much as we need them." We formed short lines for communion, dipping our frybread into the cup. A child was given a large piece.

SEVENTEEN

THE WASHITA SITE: FINDING SACRED GROUND

The Cheyenne word for the Washita River is *Hooxeeohe*, Lodge-Pole River. Events on the Washita have defined for Hart who he is and how he is to live his life. More than a lodge-pole, the Washita site represents the center pole, beginning when Lawrence was still a young chief. Hart's most oft-told, most powerful story is a conversion tale on the Washita, a chief's coming-of-age story whose tone may vary depending on the audience Lawrence is addressing. He uses the story as an anchor for his own understanding. He uses it as a cautionary tale, a parable, or a model of restorative justice in the vein of the Cheyenne peacemaking tradition.

One can learn a great deal about his development as a chief, a minister, and a person by reviewing the details of the story as Chief Hart tells it. I have heard him tell the story at least five times in various venues. I have read several published accounts. There is, of course, no replacement for his own telling, the personal element Lawrence brings to the telling, its testimonial nature. Each time I hear him tell it, I am moved to tears—for the violations we perpetrate upon one another as a human race, for the tragedies of human history—but also for the innocent and powerful act of an empathetic woman, the wisdom of traditional ways, the beauty of redemption, the richness and blessing of human community, and finally, for the power of restorative justice.

Not long after he had returned to Oklahoma, while still a young and inexperienced chief, there occurred for Lawrence a momentous event.

Chief Hart tells this story so often because he is aware of what he learned that day from his own traditions, and more than that, he recognized, perhaps for the first time, what was in store for him in his life as a peace chief.

Sometimes in the buildup to the central narrative as a prologue Chief Hart cites the teaching which was the guiding doctrine for all the old chiefs: "If you see your mother, wife, or children being molested or harmed by anyone, you do not go and seek revenge. Take your pipe. Go, sit and smoke and do nothing, for you are now a Cheyenne chief" (Hart 1981, 5). He often tries to help his audience redefine their Hollywood notion of chiefdom as power: "Being a chief is not so much to occupy a position or to perform functions but to live a way of life" (Hart, 1981, 4). Perhaps he will explain the Cheyenne phrase, *Evehonevostanehev* which means "that person is living the life of a chief" (4) to help his listeners understand. He will note for his audience that there are those who have refused to become peace chiefs because they knew they could not follow this way of life. He commends their honesty.

Sometimes when Chief Hart tells this story, he gives his audience a brief history lesson, remembering the great peace chief tradition he has inherited. He may recount the stories of great peace chiefs who would not seek revenge, White Antelope or Lean Bear, before Black Kettle. He remembers how White Antelope, realizing that the attack at Sand Creek was not a mistake, that it was, indeed, a deliberate attack, after first shouting unsuccessfully at the soldiers in English to "Stop!"—folded his arms and sang his death song, standing himself to take some of the first shots intended for his people as he sang:

Father, have pity on me. Father, have pity on me.
The old men say you have spoken truly.
Nothing lives long except the earth and the mountains.
Nothing lives long except the earth and the mountains.
(Hart 1997, 34)

The story begins on November 27, 1968, exactly one hundred years to the day from the original attack on the Washita. Chief Hart was still a relatively young and inexperienced chief trying to learn from his elders. He described himself at this time as impetuous, if not hotheaded; I imagine him filled with youthful impatience, with a sense of injustice, with determination to right the wrongs of the world!

The city of Cheyenne just a few miles from the Battle Site had indicated its wish for a commemorative reenactment of the Washita Battle. It is hard for me to imagine how those planning the event could prevail upon the Cheyenne people to agree to participate in reenacting the grisly event. Perhaps the Cheyenne people saw it as a chance to retell the story for their children, to honor these dead ancestors. Chief Hart always emphasizes the Cheyenne tribe's reluctance. Clearly, he says, the Cheyennes had no interest in celebrating a massacre:

> Not wanting to go there to celebrate a massacre, they spoke through their present-day chiefs. They would participate if two conditions were met. One, to have the proposed reenactment of the battle to be historically accurate. Second, to have unearthed remains of a victim reinterred by Cheyenne chiefs. (Hart 1981, 6)

Their first requirement of historical accuracy came back to haunt them. The demand that the unearthed remains of a Cheyenne victim killed on the Washita and still being held in the Black Kettle Museum in Cheyenne be re-interred would be the saving grace for two peoples gathered there representing both factions of the battle, for Hart and his destiny, and for justice. I believe the climactic moment foreshadowed Chief Hart's drive for restorative justice today as he has undertaken the spokesman's role for returning to the earth all native remains long forgotten on institutional shelves in this country.

As young Chief Hart understood it, the plan for the reenactment on November 27, 1968, was for the Cheyenne people to be the players of Black Kettle's original Cheyenne encampment and for the local whites to play Custer and his Seventh Cavalry. Hundreds of guests had gathered to witness the day's events, including state dignitaries. On the very grounds on which the original battle took place, Lawrence's family, including his own two young children, and other families were part of the Cheyenne encampment organized for the reenactment. However, unknown to the Cheyenne players that day, perhaps unknown to anyone but the Chamber of Commerce in the town of Cheyenne, Chief Hart emphasizes as he tells the story—another group had come into town to join in the reenactment.

During the mock attack there appeared suddenly a regiment of troops come to Oklahoma for the day from California. They called themselves "The Grand Army of the Republic, the Grandsons of the

Seventh Cavalry"—Custer's regiment. These Grandsons of Custer's Seventh came roaring up from the flank, as Lawrence remembers it. They appeared in "authentic uniforms and carried authentic weapons and their officers had authentic sabers" (Hart, 1981, 6).

He recalls that what happened as they charged was most impressive to the crowd but very threatening to the Cheyenne people. These Seventh Cavalry Grandsons played the traditional attack song, the tune known as "Garry Owen." Indeed, their forbears had attempted to use the tune "Garry Owen" one hundred years before, but the song used for attack had sputtered out when their horns froze in the terrible cold of that 1868 November dawn. These 1968 Grandsons came thundering toward the Cheyenne camp as on that earlier fateful day, "shooting blank cartridges from their authentic Spencer carbines" (Hart 1991, 61) and terrorizing the children, including Chief Hart's daughter Connie and son Nathan. As Chief Hart always says when he tells this tale, "It was too real."

Lawrence will readily admit that he was furious. The Cheyenne people felt utterly betrayed. Lawrence remembers thinking, *How do you relate to these proud Grandsons?* It was an awful scene, and Lawrence recalls his own disgust; understandably, he dreaded any personal contact with the Grandsons. It had been a historically accurate reenactment of the terror—with screams, fright, and children running. However, like the Cheyenne chiefs of earlier times, the 1968 chiefs stuck to their agreement and went into the town of Cheyenne later that day for the burial of the Cheyenne remains, the final event of the day to be carried out on the main street of the town of Cheyenne. In an act which must have felt a bit to Chief Hart like keeping faith with a broken treaty, the chiefs went in to the Black Kettle Museum, allowing the show to go on.

The chiefs, however, saw to it that the burial ceremony was done with dignity. "As the chiefs left the museum carrying a small, custom-made bronze coffin, they began chanting their special burial songs. Snow was falling as it had fallen a hundred years before" (Hart 1999, 62). Lawrence admitted the last time he told me the story that he was unable to sing with the chiefs on this occasion, for as a young chief he did not yet know the songs (Hart, Interview Sept. 6, 2005). Unbelievably, the "enemy" hounded them yet again. Recounting his own intense emotion as a young chief a full thirty years after the day, Chief Hart noted of the moment:

Over their singing the chiefs heard the command, "Present arms!" The Grandsons were there. I was there, too. "How dare they salute one their grandfathers killed!" I remember thinking. More hostile feelings emerged. (Hart 1999, 62)

It was in this moment of outrage that the mounting tensions began to be reversed by the simple traditional act of a Cheyenne woman, Lucille Young Bull. Her act would turn everything around and require that the chiefs serve the people, respond to the people, as is always their calling. The chiefs took their cue from the humblest among them. As the procession passed by her carrying the small bronze box prepared for this day, Lucille Young Bull, feeling strong emotion, Lawrence suspected, and with utter integrity, stepped out of the crowd, "took off her beautiful new woolen blanket and quickly draped it over the coffin as the procession went by" (Hart 1999, 62). She covered the box with her blanket—despite the cold and snow flurries which reminded them all of the day one hundred years earlier that they had just reenacted. It was an act of respect for a dead ancestor, an act of restorative justice for this one whose bones had been waiting on a shelf in the Black Kettle Museum—a simple, impulsive, shy perhaps, but brave act which would now force the hands of the chiefs. "As tradition dictated, the blanket would be given away" (Hart, 1999, 62).

Lawrence, a young chief accompanying the other older chiefs, knew that the blanket the woman had laid upon the burial box would need to be given away, according to tradition. Knowing that the governor of Oklahoma was in attendance that day for the event in Cheyenne, Chief Hart assumed that the blanket should be given to the Governor of Oklahoma, or some other appropriate dignitary on the scene. The old chiefs demanded that young Chief Hart step to the microphone and explain to the people that the blanket would be given away. "They may have sensed my animosity," he noted, "and decided to pull me in" (Hart, Interview Sept. 6, 2005).

When Lawrence huddled with the chiefs, they requested that Lawrence call to the microphone Captain Eric Gault, commanding officer of the Grandsons of the Seventh Cavalry. The captain came forward, stepping in sharp military fashion, drew his saber, and saluted. Lawrence himself asked the captain to do an "about face," and the blanket was wrapped around his shoulders. Lawrence no longer remembers if he was the one who placed the blanket on Captain Gault's shoulders or if it was a joint act of the chiefs as a group, including him. What he understood was that he moved in accord with the will of the chiefs who understood more than he grasped that day.

As Chief Hart wrote the story in *Mennonite Life* over a decade after it happened, he noted, "The scene that followed is one that is hard to describe. I really get emotionally caught up in it. People broke down and cried. We too cried on each other's shoulders—these grandsons of the Seventh and grandsons of Black Kettle" (Hart, 1981, 7).

I have heard Lawrence tell this story to a variety of different groups. He remembered well the first time he told the story in 1971 in Fresno, California, at a peace meeting of the General Conference Mennonite Church. It was unplanned. Peace stories were called for, and he stepped to the microphone (Hart, Interview Sept. 6, 2005). He always points to the wisdom of the old chiefs, the significance of the Cheyenne peace traditions, and what he, perhaps a somewhat impudent young chief, learned that day. Looking back again at the event for a broad Oklahoma tourist audience from his 1999 vantage point, he remarked,

> The wise Cheyenne peace chiefs had initiated a reconciliation, which resulted in conflict transformation. It was at this ceremony that the older peace chiefs indelibly impressed onto the younger what it meant to follow the instructions of Sweet Medicine, a prophet of the Cheyenne. The ceremony of reburial ended with the Grandsons firing volleys to honor the victim. There was not a dry eye in the audience. . . . When I greeted the captain of the regiment, he took the "Garry Owen" pin from his uniform and handed it to me to accept on behalf of all Cheyenne Indian people. The captain stated, "Never again will your people hear 'Garry Owen.'" (Hart 1999, 62)

I am always moved by the power of Chief Hart's refusal to analyze the story beyond his insistence that the lesson was all his. Implicit for me is the genius of the inherited Cheyenne tradition. How does one undo "what has become too real"? In this story, the old chiefs practiced what must inevitably be done according to their tradition, prayed for those who despitefully used them, gave away to those who did not deserve. They embraced the enemy as Black Kettle had embraced Major Wynkoop on the Colorado Plains, setting up a precedent. Chief Hart learned that day that one must grant faith to the one in whom one should have no trust, until that trust be reciprocated. In this way one calls out a promise from the enemy: "Never again." Eric Gault was asked to do an about face, then he was wrapped with Lucille Young Bull's blanket of love.

Chief Hart used the story to introduce the Washita Battlefield National Historic Site to the public in the tourist magazine *Oklahoma Today* in 1999. He went on to note that the Black Kettle Museum which had been constructed in the 1950s was transferred to the Oklahoma Historical Society in 1990. After the American Battlefield Protection Program was created, in 1991 State Representative Frank Lucas worked with the Oklahoma Historical Society to "spearhead growing support of local, state, and national organizations" (Hart, 1999, 62). Chief Hart remembered that the first hearing in Congress in 1994 "did not produce hoped-for results" (Hart 1999, 62).

Chief Hart's first testimonial before the congressional subcommittee to request the establishing of the Washita Battlefield National Historic Site failed. At that hearing his testimonial had emphasized the importance of the Cheyenne tradition of caring for children, pointing to the Cheyenne traditions which must be preserved. However, their request was not successful.

When Chief Hart was called to testify a second time in July 1996, he argued that the view the Cheyenne people hold about the Washita site where Black Kettle's village once stood can best be understood in the context of the Oklahoma City bombing on April 19, 1995. He recounted how he was asked to be a part of the first year's anniversary services for families of the victims, how he went onto the site, knelt on the ground, and touched the earth four times before he read the first forty-two of the 168 names of victims. He argued that "the site in Oklahoma City is hallowed ground just as the site where the village stood at Washita" (Hart 1996, 2). He commended the way the Cheyenne people had been asked to be involved in the Washita project. Not long after, the bill by Senator Don Nickles was passed and signed as public law. Today, the Washita Battlefield Site is run by the National Park Service.

In a telling article, "Sand Creek and Oklahoma City: Constructing a Common Ground," Hart drew numerous parallels between the Sand Creek massacre, which he says is "embedded in the psyche of many Cheyenne people" (1997, 33) and the Oklahoma City bombing, trying to show a contemporary readership the importance of "sacred grounds."

The grounds at the site of the Sand Creek Massacre in Colorado are venerated by Cheyenne people. The site where the Murrah Federal Office Building once stood in Oklahoma City is considered a place apart from the ordinary. The Oklahoma City assistant fire chief described the Murrah site as "a kind of holy place, for so many died there." The street in front of the site is now permanently closed as the wishes of the families of victims prevailed over merchants (Hart 1997, 34).

In this article Chief Hart argued for finding ground where people can come together on what he called "special sites" (Hart 1997, 36). He argued for ritual and the construction of "a ground that will accommodate us all" (Hart 1997, 37).

Bob Blackburn, Executive Director of the Oklahoma Historical Society, served as visionary for the Washita Battle Site project, orchestrating the players—including other visionaries, politicians, funders, local community persons, and Cheyenne leaders, among them including Chief Hart. Dr. Blackburn has great respect for Hart's ability to hear what the occasion demands, his ability to use story to move an audience, the way he "gets it" when asked to explain or defend the importance of a historical project before the varied audiences he must often address (Blackburn Interview, March 24, 2004).

Referring to the testimonials at the hearings of the subcommittees, Blackburn pointed to Chief Hart's words as instrumental in the success of the project: "It was the brilliance of Lawrence Hart, his uncanny ability to articulate what the site meant to him and his people" (Hart, Interview March 24, 2004). Interestingly, Blackburn spoke of the Washita project in almost mystical terms, recounting the close calls in his own politicking—even the weather on a particular fly in to bring dignitaries to the site—suggesting that this site's becoming a national park was "meant to be." The Washita site, even for Blackburn, seemed to have a destiny of its own. He felt fortunate to bring together and fund the various players.

Sarah Craighead was the park's superintendent at Washita during the creation of the site. In her paper about cultural resources management in the case of the Washita, she wrote, "Washita was established not only to interpret Custer's rise to fame as an Indian fighter, or to talk about the end of a way of life for native peoples, but as a place of consecration and reflection" (2004, 173). She described the management's efforts to engage the Native Americans affiliated with the park and described how the management of the park attempted to gain a tribal perspective as they put together an education program. When she spoke of the park's involvement in the Cheyenne Heritage Trail, she made clear how important Hart's work, voice, and ability to see institutional needs was for their purposes:

> The tribe had been very clear on their belief that the park's staff needed to educate the public about the Cheyenne tribe's living culture as well as the event in 1868. They also strongly believed, as did the park staff, that some of Washita's stories needed to be told with a tribal voice. In addition, we felt that it was important to interpret the Washita in context rather than as an isolated event. (Craighead, 2004, 174)

To this end, the park organizers turned to Lawrence Hart and the Cheyenne Cultural Center he had founded twenty-four years earlier. According to Craighead, it was Hart who created the concept of the Cheyenne Heritage Trail. The 420-mile route was the first Native American Cultural Route in the state of Oklahoma. It included twelve sites that interpret the Cheyenne story (Craighead 2004, 175). Craighead credits Hart's relationships with state government for allowing them to obtain the assistance of the Oklahoma Tourism Division along with the essential partnership of the Oklahoma Historical Society. It was also Hart who worked with a state senator to pass legislation directing the Oklahoma Department of Transportation to mark the trail with signage so that today 20,000 visitors per year travel some or all of the Trail. Craighead notes in her conclusions that work remains at the Washita National Historic Site, as the legislation directed that park staff return the area to its 1861 appearance—its "native environment" (Craighead 2004, 176).

If the Washita site develops as its planners hope and the Washita river valley where Black Kettle's village once camped once again supports grazing horses on the river bottom vegetation, will it not seem an act of restorative justice—as if the dry bones of the 800 ponies destroyed there in 1868 have risen in spirit to stand on sacred ground?

CHAPTER EIGHTEEN

THE CHEYENNE WAY OF JUSTICE: "COME IN AMONG THE PEOPLE"

Finally, four soldier troops [the Elk, Bowstring, Dog, and Fox] decided to go talk to him. He had been a good man in the tribe and here he was destitute. . . . They all came to Red Robe, but one or two did the talking for them all. "We are begging you to do what we ask you—we are not alone—see them all—every company among us is here. We still have your horses. Come in among the people.
—"When Two Twists Led the Cheyennes Against the Crows," by
   Stump Horn in Llewellyn and Hoebel, 1941, 3

There is a moment which stands out for me in my hours of interviewing Chief Hart these past years about his life's journey. In all the many hours we have spoken together he has been calm, unruffled, patient, analytical, not without humor, but rarely showing strong feeling. His demeanor has been one of careful deliberation and thoughtfulness, even when I have heard myself asking what must have sounded, as the words have fallen into the air, like naïve, ignorant, or insensitive questions. But in this moment I saw him angry. I sensed it as exasperation, not particularly with me, but surely including me, with the need to explain once again—after fifty years of trying—who he is, who *they* are.

Chief Hart had been introducing me to his work with the repatriation of Native remains, his service on the Review Committee for the Native American Graves Protection and Repatriation Act (NAGPRA), to which he was appointed in 1990. We had been talking about the huge number of native remains taken after the Plains battles, usually only the crania, and shipped away to museums and libraries and institutions of "science" for future study. I must have shown visible shock, perhaps even incredulity.

We had moved on to talk about his new project, which he hoped to unveil in summer 2004 at the tribal Sovereignty Symposium, an exhibit of cases in Cheyenne jurisprudence based on the classic work *The Cheyenne Way* by Karl N. Llewellyn and E. Adamson Hoebel. Suddenly he appeared to be overtaken by the incongruity, perhaps even the naïve insensitivity and ignorance of his interviewer, who certainly was guilty of needing too many obvious explanations. I can still see Chief Hart's flashing eyes as he leaned forward and looked directly at me to say, not quite in his usual measured tones:

> They were beheading us for savages on the Plains all the while we were in the possession of a longheld traditional legal code. Our people were practicing such a sophisticated system of restorative justice that it is being taught in jurisprudence classrooms today. It is of interest to judges today who find current U. S. legal systems bankrupt for creative solutions to human problems! [my paraphrase; the tape recorder was turned off].

I immediately ordered my own copy of Llewellyn and Hoebel's *The Cheyenne Way*. By the time Chief Hart called to tell me that they would open the exhibit in Oklahoma City, I had read the book and was eager to see the exhibit.

The story of Red Robe is Case 1 in *The Cheyenne Way*. Told by the Cheyenne informant Stump Horn, it illustrates how Cheyenne justice works. Summarized briefly and paraphrased, the account goes as follows. In utter anguish over the deaths of his two sons killed by the Crows, Red Robe stood in front of his lodge and called out that his horses were for the taking. He refused to keep even one to ride. The Dog Soldiers rounded up Red Robe's horses and sent an old man to see him. The messenger told Red Robe that his sons had died honorably. Why don't you take back your horses? No, Red Robe argued. Maiyun, the Supernatura,l wanted my sons to die in battle and wants that I should be afoot awhile. Red Robe was disconsolate and would not budge.

For months, Red Robe was inconsolable. When the camp moved, he was last to follow. Finally, Two Twists begged Red Robe to take back his horses. Two Twists even promised revenge upon the Crows. Thereupon, Red Robe came back into camp. Two Twists announced throughout the camp that he himself would die in the revenge. But he did not. The Cheyennes did take revenge upon the Crows. Two Twists did not die. He was honored for his good work, and the people decided he need not fulfill his vow to die. Now, Red Robe did give away horses, keeping only a few for himself. The soldiers allowed him to do so this time. Red Robe adopted Two Twists who would later be made a big chief (Llewellyn and Hoebel 1941, 3-6).

The story of Red Robe can be used as a parable of vengeance. But another underlying theme which informs this and other cases in *The Cheyenne Way* can also be seen here. The Cheyenne impulse in working justice is the restoration of each member in the tribe. Punishment for crime was often necessary, but there was a value beyond that punishment: a way should be made for each Cheyenne to "come in among the people." Community should be restored. The vilest criminal should pay for the crime but ultimately be offered a way back into community.

At the Sixteenth Annual Sovereignty Symposium in Oklahoma City, in 2003 and the year before the Sovereignty Symposium I attended, the Honorable Chief Lawrence Hart had delivered the keynote address (stepping in for Commander John Herrington, who at the last minute could not come). His title was "Cheyenne Way of Peace and Justice: The Post Lewis and Clark Period to Oklahoma Statehood"—his attempt to tie into the Symposium's theme, "From Sacagawea to Space." Hart never misses an opportunity authentically to use an assigned theme to tell stories, his own or the history of his people, to educate an audience about the deep culture of the Cheyennes. He is adept at taking an assignment and creatively and symbolically feeding into the topic the stories which give his audience new understandings in powerful anecdotal form. After he gave this particular address, the Oklahoma Supreme Court honored Chief Hart with the Friend of the Court Medal (Hart 2003, 261).

On the occasion of his address at the 2003 Sovereignty Symposium, Chief Hart had pointed to his regalia and noted that he was wearing a Thomas Jefferson Peace Medal dated 1802, three years before Lewis and Clark met the Cheyenne people in the Black Hills region not far from their sacred mountain, Bear Butte. Hart explained that Lewis and Clark handed out these medals from President Thomas Jefferson along their route, and many tribes eagerly accepted them. Not the Cheyenne. Citing historian Paul Prucha, he noted that "when [a medal] was presented to a Cheyenne chief, it alarmed him for 'he knew that the white people were all *medicine* and that he was afraid of the medal or any thing that white people gave to them'" (Hart 2003, 263).

With the reference to the medal, Chief Hart set the stage for a discussion of the treaties with the Cheyennes, the first one twenty-one years after the Lewis and Clark expedition. He discussed the betrayal of the peace chiefs and the fact that in the Sand Creek Massacre and the "so-called Battle of the Washita," the Cheyennes experienced the worst tragedies perpetrated upon Native Americans in this country. He pointed to White Antelope's martyrdom at Sand Creek as evidence of his own inheritance of a remarkable legacy.

In this particular address, Chief Hart illumined that legacy by reporting on the rediscovery of the Cheyenne way of jurisprudence. Implicit is Hart's need to show the world the genius of the Cheyenne way of doing justice. Reading that address, one can see him dreaming, visioning that a year hence he will bring the "grandfather of restorative justice Howard Zehr" (Hart 2003, 266) to the next Sovereignty Symposium to validate that the Cheyenne model is, indeed, an indigenous people's model of restorative justice to be reclaimed. He always chooses story:

> My attempt to educate others on the ways of Cheyenne justice began in the fall of 2000, when my wife and I traveled to meet some First Nations' people on the southwest side of Lake Winnipeg. On the flight from Oklahoma City to Chicago, I happened to sit across from the Honorable Robert H. Henry. . . . (Hart 2003, 264)

Judge Robert H. Henry, Shawnee, Oklahoma, was appointed to the U.S. Court of Appeals for the Tenth Circuit in 1994 by President Bill Clinton (Hart 2003, 261). Apparently Chief Hart and Judge Henry began to talk about *The Cheyenne Way* by Llewellyn and Hoebel, first published by the University of Oklahoma Press in 1941. They discussed Cheyenne justice. Further, they discussed the need for a teaching tool referencing this book so often used as "recommended reading in many law schools and conflict resolution classes across the nation." Chief Hart became project director, Judge Henry project advisor. They put together a team of legal scholars, conflict resolution specialists, and traditional Cheyenne people and peace chiefs (Hart 2003, 264).

Chief Hart described briefly some of the cases Llewellyn and Hoebel document in the text, briefly outlined the model and then announced,

> Many legal scholars are amazed that the Cheyenne chiefs practiced restorative justice. It is thought to be new. However, Llewellyn and Hoebel documented several cases when they did field work among the Cheyenne chiefs. Cheyenne chiefs practiced restorative justice long before the advent of English and United States courts, and certainly well before today's Tribal courts. (Hart, 2003, 266)

Chief Hart defined restorative justice for this group of legal experts using his friend Howard Zehr's definition, thanked Judge Henry for his advice on the project, and gave a nod to the conference theme based on Lewis and Clark's journey (which I have heard him say in other contexts is certainly nothing the Cheyenne people relish celebrating!). He made the theme his own. He transformed it with his final remarks which acknowledged the journey of Lewis and Clark and Sacagawea:

> There is another important journey. It is that of recorded case law that has made a journey from a non-literate people to educate today's law students, lawyers, judges, and justices, as well as many other life-long learners. That journey has also been most remarkable, and like Lewis and Clark's journey, it is filled with astonishment.
>
> Thanks to the "god" of Contract Law, Karl N. Llewellyn, and to the brilliant insight of a renowned anthropologist, E. Adamson Hoebel, we will be able to learn more about peace ways and restorative justice practiced by Native Americans.
>
> *Hi na ha ni.* That is all.
>
> *Hi ho.* Thank you. (Hart 2003, 267)

I was introduced to the Sovereignty Symposium a year after Chief Hart's address in summer 2004. According to the agenda provided at the meeting for the Seventeenth Sovereignty Symposium as presented by the various supporting agencies—the Oklahoma Supreme Court, The Oklahoma Indian Affairs Commission, The Indian Law Section of the

Oklahoma Bar Association, The Oklahoma Arts Council, The University of Tulsa College of Law, The University of Oklahoma College of Law, the Oklahoma City College of Law—the Sovereignty Symposium was established "to provide a forum in which ideas concerning common legal issues could be exchanged in a scholarly, non-adversarial environment." Panels developed for the event included far-ranging topics of interest to the tribes, such as "Indian Self-Determination and Tribal Self-Governance," "Policymaking Between the States and the Tribes," "The Oil and Gas Industry and Tribal Interest," "Tribal Regulation Under the Federal Environmental Statues," various panels on international interests, and many others.

The Honorable Lawrence Hart was on Panel D on Thursday, June 3, 2004: "Cheyenne Justice: An Anglo Lens and Deeper Meanings." He had flown in his good friend Dr. Howard Zehr, international expert on restorative justice and conflict transformation, to speak about the restorative justice potential of the Cheyenne cases in Llewellyn and Hoebel. One could purchase Zehr's widely read foundational primers on restorative justice in the lobby.

Lawrence as the consummate networker and storyteller delights in telling how he came to be friends with Howard. I can see that Lawrence feels both great affection and great loyalty to a friend like Howard who was there when he needed him. When Chief Hart was appointed liaison for the repatriation of Cheyenne remains from the Smithsonian Museums, he was assigned two tasks by the chiefs. First, he was to secure good tobacco for the ceremonies. Second, he was to arrange for the cedar boxes to hold the remains for burial. Lawrence went to Howard in the Mennonite Central Committee office in Akron, Pennsylvania. Howard got a huge bundle of tobacco leaves grown by the Amish and had them shipped to the Cheyenne Cultural Center.

The chiefs had assumed that the cedar boxes would be made in Oklahoma. However, they soon realized that if that were the case, the boxes would then have to be shipped to Washington, D.C. Would there be a way to get them made nearer the nation's capital city? Lawrence turned again to Howard Zehr, who put him in touch with an Amish craftsman, Emanuel "Manny" Fisher of Bird-in-Hand, Pennsylvania. Howard and his wife Ruby eventually brought the boxes Manny Fisher made to the museum in Washington, D. C. Furthermore, as a professional photographer, Howard took the still shots at the repatriation ceremonies.

Before the repatriation event, however, Howard took Lawrence to visit Manny Fisher's Amish carpentry shop. Lawrence brought the dimensions for the eighteen boxes they needed. That trip was a joy to Lawrence, who highly appreciated the ingenuity of the traditional lifestyle of the Amish. A woodworker himself, Lawrence loved Manny's shop and his excellent woodworking equipment used for making cabinets and coffins. Manny showed Lawrence around the shop among the hoses that powered the gas-run air compressors. Lawrence marveled at the quiet power. He was deeply appreciative of the care with which Manny showed him three cedar samples and allowed him to choose precisely the right color for finishing the cedar boxes. Lawrence gave Manny the dimensions. "We shook hands and that was a contract," Lawrence noted (Hart, Interview Sept. 6, 2005). I saw how Lawrence loved the genuineness of the "deal." He loved the way the Amish woodworking craft and philosophy of the Amish lifestyle fit the ceremonial need of the Cheyenne people for cedar boxes. Indeed, the preparation of the boxes was part of the restorative justice, and Manny's quiet integrity filled the bill for Lawrence.

The Fisher family was in the business of serving coach loads of people at their table where Katie, Manny's wife, cooked. After the men conducted the business of the construction of the cedar boxes, Katie invited them to her table. As it grew dark, Lawrence watched Manny light the lamps powered by propane. He later described to me the mellow glow of the lamps in the dark room. I sensed that the scene suited his Cheyenne sensibility and need for a ceremonial end to the day. Howard had become for Lawrence a much-appreciated friend who, as an expert on restorative justice, knew what Lawrence needed to restore the desecrated Cheyenne remains and intuitively understood Lawrence's own emotional needs in the process.

A special invitation was passed out in the halls where the Seventeenth Sovereignty Symposium was being held in 2004 (when I attended), welcoming participants to the Cheyenne Justice Exhibit opening and a speech by Howard Zehr. There would also be an unveiling of a sculpture by the famous Cheyenne and Arapaho bronze sculptor, Charles Pratt. The exhibit was made possible by the Cheyenne and Arapaho Tribes of Oklahoma, The Oklahoma Arts Council, the Red Moon Fund, and The Schowalter Foundation of Newton, Kansas. Chief Hart was honored that morning to bless and begin the opening ceremonies.

Before the 10:00 a.m. session, men in fatigues and berets gathered at the back of the auditorium to dance the center aisle for opening ceremonies. The drummers and singers were already gathered at the front near the long ceremonial head tables. One of the men in fatigues helped himself to the mints provided on the head table, shaking out a few from each dignitary's place so they would not be missed! Children in costume jingled by. It was clearly to be a grand parade with representatives from all the Oklahoma tribes gathering in their traditional garb in back corridors.

Chief Hart arrived in a dark blazer without a tie over which he later wore the ceremonial garb for his opening duties. Clearly he played multiple roles on this day—the peace chief who blessed the opening ceremonies, the educator who appealed to the representatives of the legal systems in Oklahoma and, I later learned, the biblical scholar who interpreted the Hebrew code and compared it to the Cheyenne legal system. He greeted the Greyhorse Singers. I was grateful to see him in a world other than the Mennonite or Cheyenne worlds in which I generally observe him. This is the world which thinks of Lawrence Hart as an "Oklahoma treasure."

The ceremony was important—not just for the tribes but for Oklahomans who present a more southern demeanor than do Kansans in this regard. Oklahomans demand ceremony, pomp and circumstance, titles and protocol. Lawrence put on his shawl to do the blessing, went to the front, and holding an eagle wing called to each of the four corners. After he finished, some tribal women warbled or lulued. He took his place at the head table.

I could see that day the importance of military history, not just for the state of Oklahoma, but for the warrior societies of the many tribes represented. There was a presentation of flags by tribal leaders. Honor guards were presented by the Vietnam Era Veterans Intertribal Association and the Kiowa Black Leggings Society. The address was given by Oklahoma's governor, the Honorable Brad Henry, "youngest presiding officer in the country," who emphasized service in his short speech. Quoting his uncle he argued that "service is the rent you pay for the space you occupy," but mostly he followed a political agenda, noting how his administration cares about the tribes. Later in the day, as a tribute to the Cheyenne Way exhibit, the governor announced the proclamation of "Cheyenne Justice Day."

The panel focused on stories from *The Cheyenne Way* and analyzed their restorative justice model and potential. Howard Zehr brought along a young protégé to apply restorative justice principles to various cases. I recognized the beauty of new ways of seeing restorative justice through the Cheyenne lens, through another culture's perspective. The discussion arrived at fundamental principles for resolving wrongdoing: creating a space for victim and offender to come together; seeking to understand the needs of those affected and the roots of the misbehavior; determining what teaching will be acceptable to all parties involved; focusing on restoration.

My lay person's sense of the Cheyenne contribution to restorative justice was clarified by the phrase used in Llewellyn and Hoebel: "Come in among the people." Wrongdoing results in expulsion from the community, but not forever. Restitution is possible. Each Cheyenne in the group was too valuable to lose. At their base, the principles of Cheyenne law evidenced reverence for life and redemption. Typically, there was no formal rule-making. Rather, a judge must always take into account intention and adjudicate case by case. Punishment was not an end in itself. Once an individual recognized and acknowledged wrongdoing, there was a move to restore that individual to membership in the group. The law was based on the tribal need for harmony and unity.

The case of Two Forks from Llewellyn and Hoebel discussed that day was instructive. The tribe was scouting buffalo. When the scouts returned, they reported where buffalo were and ordered that no one leave camp or attack until the signal was given. The hunters went out in a line together. As they topped a ridge, they saw that two men had gone ahead and were now down in the valley riding among the buffalo. For the moment, the hunters ignored the buffalo. They charged the two violators, killed their horses under the hunters, whipped the two wrongdoers, and seized and smashed their guns (Llewellyn and Hoebel, 1941, 112-113).

Two Forks, father of the two wrongdoers, now arrived on the scene. He chastised his sons for failing to obey the tribal law: "You went out alone and you did not give the other people a chance. This is what has happened to you." The chiefs also chastised them verbally—"Now you know we mean what we say." (Llewellyn and Hoebel, 1941, 112).

The restoration motif of the story is fascinating. "After that the chiefs relented. . . . They called their men to gather around. 'Look how these two boys are here in our midst. Now they have no horses and no weapons. What do you men want to do about it?'" (112) One soldier offered to give a horse from among his extra horses. Another did the same.

Bear Standing On a Ridge was the third to speak out, "Well," he announced, "we broke those guns they had. I have two guns. I will give them one." All the others said, "*Ipewa*, good." (Llewellyn and Hoebel, 1941, 113)

Ironically, when the hunters believed they had finished dealing with this deed, they looked around to find that some of their number were "way down the creek chasing bison" (Llewellyn and Hoebel, 1941, 113). They charged these wayward ones, saying that they too would receive a good whipping, but were advised not to kill their horses. "When the slackers saw them coming, Big Footed Bull, who was among them, took off the blanket he was wearing and spread it on the ground. It was one of those fine Hudson's Bay blankets which the governments used to issue to Indians" (113).

This time the hunters dismounted and divided the blanket, tearing it into long strips for the culprits to wear as tail pieces when they danced, then cut an ear off each of the culprits' horses! Llewellyn and Hoebel note: "The duty of all the members of a society to participate in the administration of punishment and the liability of all members to discipline in case of neglect were stated by all informants as generalized rules and are borne out in several cases" (113).

Lawrence closed the panel discussion at the Seventeenth Sovereignty Symposium by showing how the Hebrew tradition dovetails with Cheyenne justice. There was a sense in which he was returning those of us in the audience to an uncorrupted, more innocent look at the good news. He noted that neither the Hebrew nor the Cheyenne models of justice is Anglo. As usual, he was seeking to restore these texts to some unpolluted ground. He compared Mt. Moriah and Bear Butte, noting that the oral history tells the Cheyenne people that their way of being was delivered from on high by children.

I was reminded again of the power of ceremony and symbol to convey understanding as I listened to the accounts of Cheyenne justice. In the story of Two Forks, when the men tore the blanket into strips to be used to dance, the power of the wrongdoing would continue to shame the warriors whose horses' ears had been cut off—so that all in the community might remember. Who knows what ceremony says? It does not say; it means.

Whenever he can, Hart speaks for the power of ceremony and ritual. For example, in his article discussing the parallels between Sand Creek and Oklahoma City on the need for constructing common ground, he offers this side note to his own denomination:

> I have noted with interest and satisfaction that use of ritual is increasing in Anabaptist worship services, and it seems women are leading this paradigm shift. Use of ritual may be a twentieth century reformation that will truly create a priesthood of all believers. (Hart, 1997, 37)

The opening of The Cheyenne Justice Exhibit was planned for the noon hour and began with the traditional Cheyenne blessing invoked to the four cardinal directions. The little tepees on the head table were made by Lawrence's granddaughter's class in school. Lawrence was Master of Ceremonies and the Honorable Robert H. Henry gave opening remarks. Howard Zehr gave a short introduction to the concept of restorative justice. The exhibit was artfully done, with Lawrence himself having built, during the past winter, the beautiful cedar stands which held the exhibit. The very act of construction served as the kind of hands-on servanthood symbolic of the peace chief.

Art, symbol, ceremony, and teaching are so interlinked in Cheyenne culture that I was not surprised that an important part of this ceremony was the unveiling of a bronze by the renowned Cheyenne and Arapaho sculptor Charles Pratt. Women and especially children were called upon to come to help with the unveiling. To teach and instruct, the Cheyenne Justice Exhibit gave an artful presentation of the historical Cheyenne cases, the simple and lyric stories of Cheyenne justice offered for consideration in a beautiful presentation of wood, painting, feathers, symbols—all designed with the Cheyenne cardinal directions in mind.

Later that day, I was alone with the exhibit when the workers came to clean up the chairs in Ballroom E. They were intrigued. They walked around the exhibit and read the stories, as I was doing, all of us quiet and thoughtful as we read the provocative questions and insights. As we wandered near one another, we began to talk about justice as we had experienced it. The men were in awe of the stories, filled with hope and questions. They had experiences with prison and the law. They wanted to talk about our broken system. We shared what we knew.

I kept turning over in my mind the description Howard Zehr had given us in his remarks that day pointing to a justice model which is "not on the cutting edge but on the healing edge." I could not forget the story of Two Twists told to Llewellyn and Hoebel by Stump Horn. The warriors went out to Red Robe, intent on finding a way to bring him back into the community and begged of him, "We still have your horses. Come in among the people" (3).

CHAPTER NINETEEN

BURYING THE DEAD

To the Cheyennes the real soul or spirit of a person was called the Ma'tasooma. At death the soul separated itself from the body and traveled across Seozemeo, the Milky Way, to Se'han, the place of the dead, where the deceased was reunited with those who had gone before. Here all dwelled happily, close to the presence of Maheo, very much as they had on earth. They had fine white lodges, plenty of buffalo to hunt, fast horses, and an abundance of the good things of life. Only suicides and the very bad were barred from this peaceful existence. There was no hell or punishment after death; wrongdoing was atoned for during this life by enduring both the punishment meted out by the tribe and the ostracism of tribal members. Goodness and rightness were sought for their own sake and for the approval of one's fellow beings; recognition, honor, and positions of respect and leadership provided strong motivations for people to whom material wealth meant little.
—Chalfant 1989, 313

Nearly every time I came to visit the Cheyenne Cultural Center for an interview or even began by telephone to make arrangements to talk with Lawrence, he mentioned that he was planning for a funeral somewhere in the seventy-mile radius of former mission churches. Sometimes he travels much farther, depending upon where his constituents have moved. In fact, "burying the dead" is an important theme in his life's work.

As he conducts these services, I see him again as one who erects the axis mundi, the symbol he spoke of in his Bethel College commencement address—that center pole raised between this earth in this time and another time. If he is himself to be compared to the center pole used in the Cheyenne re-creation of the earth, one sees that the hole dug deep into the earth in which he stands is a foundation which goes down into the past and allows him to stand firm for many of us as the connection between this earth and the next life, assisting us in that passage and, most importantly, keeping the worlds connected.

I see him as that center pole now, as I could not have seen him that day that I stood in the Bergthal cemetery outside Corn, where so many members of my daddy's family have been buried.

The day I remember was at least a decade ago, when I knew Lawrence Hart only as an important name. He stood before us that day in the wind above the open grave of my Aunt Ruth on land her ancestors had given to the church for a burial plot. Reverend Hart had served as an interim pastor in the First Mennonite Church in Clinton to which Aunt Ruth belonged. And on that day he conducted her funeral service.

I stood beside her burial plot watching a meadowlark, the sky, the horizon, Reverend Hart's words only partly penetrating my consciousness. I was thinking about the land, the way we lay claim to the land. God knows, the Hinz family has fought over the land, who should lay claim to an inheritance, as have so many rural families—Mennonite, Cheyenne, and others. But that day I was thinking that the land in which we lay our dead, this ground on which I was standing, may be the only land we have any right to, these small marked plots where our dead lie. Because we return here, tell their stories, remember them, perhaps this is the land we need.

Somehow when Lawrence said the words that day so often spoken to lay someone to rest in the soil, "The Lord giveth and the Lord taketh away; blessed be the name of the Lord," I felt heartsick for all of us. Was it because the words came from the mouth of Reverend Hart, Cheyenne and Mennonite, that I heard them differently? The text Hart used that day reminded me of what our peoples have shared—faith and land. What else do we share as peoples? Death. The burial of our dead.

When the committal service was over, we watched as Aunt Ruth joined the others in the old country cemetery. We walked again past the old markers, the long dead. My cousin had recently told me the story of coming to this cemetery some months earlier, accompanying her father after a funeral to bury an old German Mennonite cousin. As the procession had mounted the hill, they saw, standing at attention over his grave, the dead man's horse, the horse he had so loved while still an active horseman in his final weeks. It was years and many stories later that I learned that a traditional Cheyenne burial practice included killing a man's best horse near his grave or under the tree which contained his scaffolding.

Lawrence Hart buries the dead for his people. Recently, when I arrived at the Cheyenne Cultural Center, I noticed that Chief Hart was tired. I knew he had had cataract surgery on both eyes. I probed, asking questions about his intense travel schedule. He then began to tell me about the services he had conducted for a wonderful old Cheyenne woman who had lived to be ninety-one, whose Cheyenne name, *Ah mi yo ni i,* translates to Trail Woman.

When Trail Woman or Katherine Nibbs Bull Coming was a teenager in the Fonda Community, she was baptized by the Mennonite missionary G. A. Linscheid. She was a member of the Seiling Mennonite Church when she died, having over the years moved from Fonda along with other Cheyenne people who began moving from their allotted lands into Seiling (Hart, Interview Oct. 20, 2004).

Katherine's husband had also been a member of the local Mennonite church. Lawrence and pastor Clifford Koehn had conducted his service some twenty years earlier. He was buried in Cantonment, the old cemetery established by the Mennonites. It was well-known that Katherine's wishes were for her service to follow the pattern set by the service for Roy Bull Coming. Koehn called Lawrence to have the sermon.

Lawrence did what he always does to prepare for these services. He researched the Mennonite church records he holds at the Cheyenne Cultural Center to learn more about Katherine. Generally, Lawrence knows that when a baptism occurred in the early years, after instruction in a catechism class, an entire group was baptized. He likes to mention the names of group members at a funeral service. But Katherine was alone on the day of her baptism, Lawrence learned from the records. So he could not mention names of the others she was baptized with so those in the audience could nod and make their own connections.

When he gave the sermon for Trail Woman that day he did mention, however, that missionary G. A. Linscheid would likely have conversed with the Cheyenne people and with Katherine in her own language. The catechism instructions were probably in English, as was the teaching manual. But Lawrence said in his sermon that Linscheid knew enough Cheyenne—certainly the words for God, Jesus Christ, other key theological concepts—to teach Katherine the concepts which would have made her comfortable with her belief system (Hart, Interview Oct. 20, 2004).

When I asked Lawrence about the details, he noted that there was a huge crowd for Katherine's service, held at the local Methodist church because of its larger capacity. The church was filled, and people stood on the sides, in the back, into the hall. When the ministers accompanied Katherine's body outside, he saw that some people were in the hall and some outside. There was such a long line, in fact, that the viewing took an hour. In such a case, Lawrence noted, the people want to greet the ministers and shake hands. "I probably shook hands with 400 people at her services."

Knowing he would have a large audience, Lawrence had spent considerable time preparing his message. He used favorite passages from the Old and New Testaments, still trying to keep his remarks to less than twenty minutes. "I always know that the family members are very tired after the physical demands of an all-night wake in the home, such as Katherine had."

I interrupted Lawrence then, curious to know whether the wake, which I think of as an Irish Catholic tradition, is a feature of traditional Cheyenne funeral practice. No, Lawrence told me, the wake was introduced here by the Mennonites. And the Cheyenne people continue to practice that tradition? Yes, he said, because it is a time when people can gather to speak about the loved one lost and to share memories, a communal event. Therefore, at the service itself, the speaking is left to the ministers. Usually today wakes do not last all night, Lawrence commented—maybe only until ten in the evening when the funeral directors come and take the body. But often even after the body is taken back to the funeral home there are refreshments and good visiting well into the night.

I was curious to know whether Lawrence used the Cheyenne language in Katherine's service. Yes, he answered, because people like to hear some Cheyenne from the Bible as well as phrases important to them, phrases that comfort them. Lawrence revealed then that where applicable he also incorporates into his sermons the traditional thinking of the Cheyenne people before their contact with missionaries. The Cheyennes were convinced, Lawrence said, that there was a place for the dead in the Milky Way. Thus the dead would travel on a journey to the Milky Way. He always reminded his audience that this heaven is where Jesus went to prepare a place for us. He is the Way, also translated as the Road—a Trail. "The English terms *road* and *path* are used by Cheyennes to indicate that a person is following a particular design or recipe for living" (Moore 1996, 181).

Lawrence liked the way the biblical texts fit the services for Katherine or Trail Woman. He told his audience it was fitting that here they had come together for the death of Trail Woman, now traveling on her own trail to the place prepared for her where her husband and others had gone ahead. I was thinking of that oft-quoted passage, "I am the way, the truth, and the life." There are many texts for the road, the way, the trail, which can take a person on a journey to the heavens, the Milky Way.

Lawrence explained to me that even as he assured the attenders that Trail Woman was now on her journey, he also likes to use two well-known Cheyenne phrases the older people especially treasure. The first phrase is *Zi o vo ssi dan ni, i di sshi pi vi ah mo kho vi ssta vi,* "The person has gone on her journey in a good way." That phrase should be said at a service such as Katherine's. The second phrase is *Hi yah i i sshi vo mah zi yo o,* "Perhaps they have seen each other again." He was referring here, Lawrence explained, to her relatives who had gone on before.

I saw in Reverend Hart's ministrations at a burial the way he stands between the two worlds. "The Lord giveth and the Lord taketh away; blessed be the name of the Lord"—that text he used to bury my Aunt Ruth years ago. And now, "Trail Woman has gone on her journey in a good way . . . perhaps they have seen each other again."

After the long line of viewing, what happened next? Everyone at the service followed the procession in automobiles to the cemetery, Lawrence said, in this case to that historic old cemetery at Cantonment, for a brief burial, a Cheyenne song, some Scripture, and prayer. Lawrence did the final committal because he speaks Cheyenne. The name of the one being buried should be spoken in Cheyenne. Trail Woman . . . has gone on her journey in a good way. . . .

And, the long day, how does the day get so long?

In our tradition, it is the family who feeds the visitors. In other churches, not Cheyenne, I realize that the congregation provides the meal—a good practice. In our practice, the family feeds the visitors. In my observation, that is highly therapeutic. The family is always concerned about preparing the meal. Many of them do it themselves. So, they are busy all during the time before the services, planning their meal. They're baking. They get up early. And in their busy-ness, in the kitchen preparing, they talk about the person just lost. And there is humor, as they remember that person. Generally, this is a huge meal. Of course, there were lots of people to work on this meal for Katherine. Close friends offer to help. (Hart, Interview Oct. 20, 2004)

Was it a traditional meal? There were traditional mainstays, Lawrence said, including beef soup and corn soup made with dried corn. The people like that dried corn soup, he noted. Also, there is usually a special cracker. It reminds Lawrence of hard tack, something used in the old days.

Later that evening, Betty brought me a package of the chowder crackers typically served at a Cheyenne funeral. Betty explained that for a number of years they could not buy the cracker, but it has become available again. Nabisco makes the "famous chowder cracker" whose brand name is Crown Pilot. It is heavy and solid, like tradition, and includes cottonseed oil, molasses, and barley flour among its ingredients.

When I did a quick check on the history of the Crown Pilot cracker on Nabisco's web site and found the Kraft food timeline, I learned that in 1792 John Pearson established America's first commercial bakery in Newbury Port, Maine, to make "pilot bread," a tough and durable biscuit to sustain sailors.

Once again I note that the Cheyenne love of traditional ways serves not only as an ethic, as in the case of the old chiefs who were led to reconciliation by their need to give the blanket away after the Washita reenactment, but also as historical preservation. Cheyenne funeral meals today include the Crown Pilot chowder cracker, a descendant of an early American biscuit.

Betty further explained that the beef soup eaten with the Crown Pilot chowder cracker involves a distinctive Cheyenne preparation maintained from earlier times. Beef or venison is sliced very thin and dried in the hot sun. The dried beef is boiled with salt pork to make a broth for drinking. The thin strips of meat are eaten along with fry bread, perhaps. Of course, the dried meat is in demand, especially by the older persons in the tribe. It is tedious to make. Therefore, it is given as a gift, especially to the elderly.

Does Cheyenne tradition for funeral foods include desserts? I wanted to know, thinking of the traditional Mennonite pies served at funerals. According to Lawrence, a Cheyenne meal following a funeral might include cake. As earlier mentioned, rice and raisins were once commodity items given out by the Indian Agency and the mixed dish of rice and raisins has become part of a Cheyenne traditional feast.

The funeral service of Trail Woman had concluded with a significant Cheyenne tradition. After the women set up the food, the people went through a cafeteria style line. Following prayer, the family had prepared the traditional giveaway. They gave away new goods—shawls, lots of Pendleton blankets, very expensive, that the family had procured for this purpose. The Pendleton blanket is an item treasured by the Cheyennes. It replaced the old Hudson Bay blanket used in trade. Lawrence and Betty offer for sale and display at the Cheyenne Cultural Center a few samples of the Pendleton blankets in the old patterns and colors. A Pendleton blanket costs about $150.

To whom were these goods given? I wanted to know. The family, I learned, prepares a list of those to whom they wish to give. In Seiling, at Trail Woman's service, Lawrence had been the first one called forward. The gifts were clearly a way of showing gratitude for Reverend Hart's help. There were gifts for the women who helped cook. There were gifts for Katherine's friends. The giveaway was the final event of the funeral ceremony.

I realized as I listened to Lawrence describe the traditional Cheyenne funeral that I did not even know how to correctly spell *giveaway*, a term not generally in use in my vocabulary. I have to consider when I write it whether to use one word or two, whether to hyphenate. When I thought of my Mennonite ancestors, I realized that Lawrence was right to use the passage we have probably overemphasized: "The Lord giveth and the Lord taketh away. Blessed be the name of the Lord." My dictionary defines the word *giveaway* exactly wrong—"something given free or sold cheap to attract customers." That sense differs greatly from the beautiful expensive Pendleton blankets bought and given away, first to the minister—a peace chief who comforted the family using the words of the Cheyenne language first taught to Trail Woman by a German Mennonite missionary, to pronounce in Cheyenne that Trail Woman had gone on her journey in a good way!

Later, it was Betty who schooled me in the concept of the giveaway. It is primarily practiced at chiefs' feasts, funerals, and pow wows. The point of the giveaway is to publicly honor and show respect to the recipient. Betty remarked that the giving should be done in a spirit of humility. "If you want to give," Betty says, "try to do it without public showiness. You might even take it to the family." She agreed that giving can also be a way of redistributing property. If she has several samples of a certain item and she knows that someone else might need such an item, she finds a way to give.

CHAPTER TWENTY

RETURN TO THE EARTH

It is less well known or simply unacknowledged that cultural customs regarding the earth practiced by Native Americans have parallels in both the Old and the New Testament. One that immediately comes to mind each time I see a Cheyenne traditionalist touch the earth ceremonially is Psalm 24:1. The psalmist declares that—

> *The world and all that is in it belong to the Lord,*
> *The earth and all who live on it are his. (TEV)*

The ritual of a Cheyenne traditional priest touching the earth four times is an acknowledgement that the earth is a creation of God and a part of the circle of life. . . . [O]ne cannot conduct an action or speak without first acknowledging the earth to be a part of being.
—Hart, "The Earth Is a Song Made Visible" in Redekop, 2000

In "Connections Past, Present and Future," the 1998 address Hart delivered at Bethel College, he developed the concept of the axis mundi, the sacred center pole the Cheyenne people use in their renewal of the earth ceremony. A cottonwood tree erected in the center of the medicine lodge serves as a symbolic center of the earth where God and humanity meet. Chief Hart referred to the axis mundi to bring his speech to a climax. He announced his presence on stage, an emissary from the Cheyenne territories many years after the college's first president, C. H. Wedel, had come from the Darlington Indian School on these same

Cheyenne and Arapaho lands to lead the college. It was, for him as well as for many of us in his audience, an awe-inspiring moment. He proclaimed, "This is an axis mundi."

Lawrence Hart had found sacred ground where he stood that day as he sensed the divine hand guiding two peoples across continents and centuries. However, after the moment's hush, he moved quickly toward the speech's end with a postscript on the Cheyenne connection to the earth. Such a move is characteristic in Hart's speechmaking.

To exemplify the significance of the earth for Cheyenne theology, Chief Hart described the translation of the classic German Christmas hymn, "Silent Night," into the Cheyenne language. He noted that the hymn composed in 1818 in German and later translated into English has no reference to the earth in either language. But when Rodolphe Petter translated the hymn into Cheyenne with the help of his Cheyenne informant Harvey White Shield, the Cheyenne word for earth, *ho 'e va*, entered the text. "The language informants must have thought, 'How can one sing a hymn of incarnation without reference to the earth?' The full richness of the incarnation, its deep and profound meaning, is captured when the word 'ho 'e va' is used by a people whose culture is inextricably connected to the earth," Chief Hart explained.

Then he closed his address with a blessing, a line from a Harvey White Shield song which has been translated from Cheyenne to English and is used all over the world in the *Mennonite Hymnal* today: "Let your love come on down and touch your children here on earth." This line of the song is another image for the axis mundi—the connection between earth and heaven.

Singing respect for the earth is a very old Cheyenne tradition. Chief Hart described in his essay, "The Earth Is a Song Made Visible," the ritualistic singing so typical of Native Americans. They traditionally sang for seasonal tasks of tilling, planting, harvesting—and for the stages of human life—being born, the various activities of life, and dying (Redekop, 2000, 174).

The most sacred ceremony for the Cheyennes, variously known as the Sun Dance or Medicine Lodge ceremony, is a recreation of the world. Creating the altar in the medicine lodge involved bringing in elements which represented the whole earth:

> On the altar were the paramount things of the earth, including a
> buffalo skull, strips of sod to represent the four cardinal direc-

tions and the sun, and the foliage of useful vegetation such as cottonwoods and plum bushes. The lodge itself referred to the heavens, and appropriate designs were applied there. Bundles of vegetation were tied to the center pole, and dried buffalo meat was secured to one of the bundles by a broken arrow. To this, a rawhide image of a human was also attached. . . . Dancers were painted five times during the fifth and sixth days of the ceremony with colors (yellow, pink, white, black) and designs (the sun, moon, flowers, plants) that referred to the blessings of the earth. (Comer, 1996, 67-68)

The event was, literally, a recreation of the entire earth's bounty, including the human place within it. Required attendance by all members of the Cheyenne tribe suggested that each member must annually recommit allegiance to the earth, for the year ahead could hold dire consequences for one who would not attend. Literally, the reenactment produced "good medicine." The spectacle of the ritual ceremonies bound the tribe together and moved them to joint commitment and behavior.

The major project which has consumed much of Chief Hart's time and energy since 1990 has been christened "Return to the Earth," a repatriation project which seeks to accord respect to the long-unburied remains of Native American people by placing them into and restoring them as members of the earth. The repatriation effort is a massive restorative justice project, intertribal and inter-denominational, which Chief Hart has undertaken with the intent of burying the thousands of unidentified (with regard to tribal affiliation) remains. The Scripture text which often accompanies the literature around this project is from the Old Testament prophet, Nehemiah 2:3b: "Why should my face not be sad, when the city, the place of my ancestors' graves, lies waste and its gates have been destroyed by fire?"

Chief Hart became involved in this repatriation project when selected in 1993 by Edward Wilson from the National Museum of Natural History as a liaison to the Cheyenne people. Hart was asked to help gather tribal leaders to discuss the repatriation of the eighteeen Cheyenne remains that the Museum held. He agreed, gathering leaders of the Cheyenne people in a tepee on land adjacent to the Cheyenne Cultural Center, where they met with Dr. Thomas Killion of the National Museum. As they talked, Killion described for the gathering of tribal leaders the Museum's intent to ship the crania packed in Styrofoam pieces in cardboard boxes to Oklahoma. Imagining such a process, the Cheyenne leaders were incensed at what they deemed callous and insensitive treatment of the remains. Open hostility broke out.

Chief Hart tried to keep everyone talking. "Chairman Wilson has asked you to talk," he remembered telling his fellow Cheyenne leaders, "and you have agreed that you would do so." He guided them back to the goal. Eventually, the Cheyenne tribal leaders did continue to discuss the repatriation of remains, and they made some decisions together. They decided they would find their own funds, make their own burial boxes, perform their own ceremonies. They would bring their own people back to Oklahoma themselves. They discussed the fact that the burial boxes should be made of cedar; they imagined how they might sing and pray over them ceremonially; they chose tribal delegates to go to the museum and retrieve the remains. They instructed Chief Hart to follow their discussions by finding the means to repatriate and helping them to realize the particulars of the burials. Chief Hart turned to his friend Howard Zehr, who helped to put him in touch with Manny Fisher, the Amish craftsman who then made the eighteen cedar boxes according to the tribe's specifications.

Channel 5 News of KOCO-TV, an ABC affiliate in Oklahoma City, reported in several nightly segments on the Cheyenne tribe's sojourn to Washington, D.C., its mournful gathering of Cheyenne remains which had been retained there, the ceremonial ministrations, and the trek back to Oklahoma for burial . The segments were eventually gathered into a video, "Long Journey Home," a powerful documentary giving the burial national exposure. That specific Cheyenne burial continues today to serve as a model for other tribes' repatriation events. In the course of only four months the Cheyenne tribe returned their ancestors to the earth.

I heard Chief Hart's presentation at a national gathering of the Mennonite church in Nashville, Tennessee, several years ago as he began to lay out the needs for the repatriation project. I was astonished by his demeanor as he spoke to that audience revealing the fact that there existed thousands of remains, mostly crania, of native peoples on the shelves of museums and universities in this country. Without obvious bitterness, embracing both victim and offender, Chief Hart described the 1860 orders of U.S. Army General Otis to frontier medical personnel to collect the remains of Native Americans. The remains were to be shipped to the Army Medical Museum in Washington, D.C., for scientific study of the crania size. In addition, the ongoing development of weaponry, specifically the rifle, called for such a review in the eyes of the military.

Chief Hart described the 1989 National Museum of the American Indian Act that mandated the Smithsonian Institution Museums to repatriate human remains, the 1990 Native American Graves Protection and Repatriation Act (NAGPRA). He noted that following the death of William Tall Bull, a member of the review committee for overseeing the Act, settling disputes, and reporting to Congress, Chief Hart himself was selected to serve on the review committee. Lawrence once told me that he had heard Bill Tall Bull say, "I want all remains off the shelves and buried." Lawrence took up that mantle.

The Return to the Earth project was based in the Mennonite Central Committee (MCC)-U.S. Peace and Justice Ministries. Hart challenged this body with an 1864 photo of peace chiefs passing by a church, looking for sanctuary. He used the photo to symbolize the silence of the Christian church with regard to atrocities like the Sand Creek Massacre so many years ago. Hart pled with his own peace denomination, the Mennonite church, to take up the challenge of restoring justice through the burial of these remains.

Then he widened the circle. He realized there would need to be regional burial sites around the country. MCC-U.S. Peace and Justice Ministries committed to raise money to secure four acres in the Midwest for a cemetery to bury 20,000 remains. Chief Hart formed a working committee for the project, including representatives from the Council of Native American Ministries (CoNAM), the Council for American Indian Ministry (CAIM), the voice for American Indians with the United Church of Christ, and the Conference of Religions for Peace, UN Church Center in New York City. Other denominational groups continue to join in the effort as Chief Hart negotiates this massive project, interceding among the federal government, the tribes, the denominations, and their theologies, the various regions—to find sites and keep the massive project slowly moving.

When we talked about the particulars of putting together the Midwest site adjacent to the Cheyenne Cultural Center at Clinton, Oklahoma, I began to see Lawrence's vision for a restorative justice project emerging. Tribal leaders would take the lead in ceremonial events, making sure there was a proper burial, appropriate singing, grieving those who had been desecrated when they had not been properly laid to rest. But the participation of non-tribal Mennonites was also important to restore justice. Mennonites and other denominational representatives across the country would make cedar boxes with their own tools in their own workshops—a bit like some families build their own caskets, praying and remembering while they work. Mennonite architects and carpenters would help build a ceremonial building at the burial site to prepare the remains. Church people, including children who were not builders, could cut the lengths of cloth to wrap the remains. Touching with their own hands the cedar and the cloth, Mennonites and other Christians could "touch" the grief and the wrong; they could attend and observe the return to the earth by native peoples. They could feel the return of power and dignity. They could participate in restorative justice. It would be a way for the church to break its silence.

Pondering Chief Hart's leadership role in the Return to the Earth project allows me a chance to comment on the leadership of a contemporary peace chief. I felt it to be almost a paradoxical question to ask Lawrence about the *authority* of contemporary chiefs. I know well from observing his life that a peace chief commands respect. I also know the chief practices a form of servant leadership. I can see by observing Chief Hart's role in the Return to the Earth project that a peace chief leads— that is, he does what needs to be done according to his own judgment, the discernment of the chiefs in counsel with one another, and the will of the Cheyenne people. But I did ask Lawrence to talk about the authority of the modern-day chiefs, an awkward question for him.

He began by giving me a history lesson. Starting with the Indian Reorganization Act (IRA) of 1934, a council form of government was standardized among the Indian tribes. Prior to that, when the Indian agents came to visit a tribe, they found that each had a different form of government. For that reason the Bureau of Indian Affairs (BIA) mandated a council form of government with bylaws in place according to a BIA model. Among the tribes the traditional systems were thus replaced with the new BIA system. Since that time, Lawrence noted, the Cheyenne people have had two systems. Of course, the older people, all gone now, much preferred the traditional Cheyenne system. In Oklahoma, the Thomas Rogers Oklahoma Indian Welfare Act replaced the IRA model. According to that model, some chiefs were elected according to the pre-

scribed council form of government. Yet the Cheyenne people continued to maintain the traditional chieftain system they had known for so
many years.

Lawrence acknowledged that the traditional chief's role as moral
leader is still crucial. The contemporary chief acting as a servant to his
people, especially in the discernment of their needs, is much valued.
Lawrence has taken seriously his role as chief in discerning the will of the
Cheyenne people—beginning with his 1970s role as chair of the fifteenth Business Committee, when he traveled the country to talk with
the people about how to program the funds they would receive from the
government. That need to "discern the will of the people" is balanced by
the chief's vision and leadership and his entitlement to exert moral authority, as Chief Hart has done, for example, in relation to the repatriation project. Thus the chief's role today appears to embody the age-old
dance of true leadership: exerting moral authority and vision while at
the same time listening to and responding to the will of the people.

Lawrence emphasized the advisory role of today's traditional chief.
He noted that under the tribe's constitution, every quarter the tribal
council is to invite the chiefs and hear them in their advisory capacity.
Beyond that, the Cheyenne people maintain their traditional council
wherein the chiefs serve as mediators, advisers, and settle family disputes—among other mediating roles. The chiefs continue to model servanthood as their predecessors taught them to do. In a feast for the people, chiefs still wait to be the last to be served. However, they are honored
at a community dance: after the opening anthem, the first dance is the
dance of honor for the chiefs.

One role of the chiefs Lawrence takes seriously is training new leaders. He notes that typically they replace a deceased chief only after waiting a year or more. Meanwhile, they carefully seek a new chief with specific traits. Lawrence mentioned among those traits honesty, generosity,
leadership qualities, the behaviors of a good family man, and good
moral character.

When the chiefs ask a new candidate to become a chief, they allow
him time to consult with his nuclear family. Every chief will talk to him.
Then he sets a time to invite the chiefs for a final talk, to encourage him.
This process is very deliberate. The candidate smokes as a pact or vow.
There is ceremonial drumming and singing, and the new chief dances
with the old chiefs.

The feast and giveaway required of the new chief is important as a sign of the chief's commitment. It may take a while before the new chief and his family can gather what they need to give away and make arrangements for the feast. Lawrence acknowledged that this collection of goods on the part of the new chief may take a year or two (Hart, Interview Sept. 6, 2005).

Mentoring younger chiefs into the chief's role has long been important to the traditional chiefs. As an older chief now, this role is especially important to Chief Hart. He noted the example of Jacob All Runner, one of the old chiefs who spoke with Lawrence about the chief's role when Lawrence was being initiated. Jacob All Runner was brought in as a "kid chief" at perhaps age nine, Lawrence believed, and served until he died in his eighties.

When I questioned him about the role of the modern-day traditional chief, Lawrence had participated the previous weekend in feasts and giveaways offered by two new chiefs. There the older chiefs had discussed their mentoring role and questioned four young candidates, each ten to twelve years old, as they sought "kid chiefs" who could be mentored. Lawrence said that the old chiefs were so impressed with this group of four young men that they took them all in! He marveled at how well they answered the questions posed to them. I asked Lawrence what qualities the chiefs were looking for in the young boys. "We want to see that a boy appreciates his grandparents, that he listens, that he has an interest in Cheyenne ways" (Hart, Interview Sept. 6, 2005).

I prodded Lawrence to do what he is reluctant to do—comment on his own role as a chief. He noted that it has been an exciting and fulfilling role. Just as quickly, he acknowledged that he has always set parameters on what his Christian stance permits. For example, he has always made some choices about what he can or should do in the traditional Sun Dance. He adds that it has brought him great satisfaction to participate in the traditional Sun Dance to the extent that he has done so.

He was thoughtful a moment before he said that, for him, the greatest satisfaction has come through the chief-as-servant role. Today, for example, those who serve on the Business Committee for the Cheyenne tribe receive a handsome salary. Lawrence did his work for the tribe in the 1970s completely *gratis*.

Lawrence acknowledged that his work and decisions have not always pleased everyone in the tribe. He has been accused of syncretism.

He has been judged to be too much aligned with the white world—with regard to faith and other issues. I know he has experienced disappointment when there is dissension within the tribe, as there is bound to be. I know from a non-tribal source that there has been a split in the tribe related to who is today the Keeper of the Arrows. Lawrence will not discuss this with me—some topics are off-limits, but it is clear that the dissension brings him great pain.

Both adults and younger people question Chief Hart's strong loyalty to his Christian faith. He is in dialogue continuously with various persons over the appropriation of indigenous songs—even the Mennonite appropriation of Harvey Whiteshield's hymn in the *Mennonite Hymnal.* He is asked to interpret Harvey Whiteshield: was he both Cheyenne and Christian? He must constantly try to discern the appropriate way to walk this boundary line between his Cheyenne identity and his chosen faith. Eventually, however, Lawrence concluded our conversation with confidence, "I look at my models, those who went before me on this issue. On the question of being both Cheyenne and Christian, that question has been settled. For me that was settled by our grandparents" (Hart, Interview Sept. 6, 2005).

Pastoring a church brings its own sets of failures and disappointments. Of course, Lawrence wishes there were more baptismal candidates. Nearby Cheyenne Mennonite communities tell him they need a new church. But where are the people, he asks? Maintaining a community of believers in his own Koinonia Church, like so many of the rural and small-town congregations throughout the larger Mennonite church along with other denominations, sometimes seems nearly impossible. The old faithful pass on; the children move away; the community declines; the remnant of believers grows thin.

TWENTY-ONE

THE SUN DANCE

"*T*his is our grandfather," *Chief Hart said, cautioning the large group of Cheyenne men, the warrior societies, as they prepared to pull the ropes. They were about to raise its long height skyward at the same time that they thrust the tree's trunk deep into the hole in the earth. It was a dark night mid-July under the stars where members of the Cheyenne tribe had set up camp in the pasture near El Reno, Oklahoma, for the Sun Dance ceremonies. This is the tree that Chief Hart had carefully chosen, walking the earth in search of a perfectly straight cottonwood with at least forty rings. This is the anchor for the prayer lodge, the "grandfather," which rises toward heaven and to which will be attached the lesser poles to form the sacred circle of the lodge. The prayers of the people this night depend upon its strength, its rising straight into the dark night sky with hundreds of prayer cloths somehow miraculously attached; all of us waited, holding our breath, to watch them rise toward the heavens.*

The Sun Dance, as the foremost annual ceremony performed by the Cheyennes, is seen as a re-creation of the earth. In fact, the Cheyenne word for the dance, *Oxheheom,* means "new life" or "world renewal" ceremony. Traditionally a vision quest ceremony called for by a sponsor, it was and is a communal event for the Cheyenne people. In the past, as they became separated into bands and extended families, all were expected to come together for this special occasion.

The ceremony is also known as the "medicine lodge ceremony," and the construction of the Sun Dance lodge reenacts the creation of the world. For example, when the tribal chiefs address the tree which has been cut, words spoken over it might be such as these:

> The whole world has picked you out this day to represent the world. We have come in a body to cut you down, so that you will have pity on all men, women, and children who may take part in this ceremony. You are to be their body. You are to represent the sunshine of the world. (Comer quoting Berthrong 1999, 67)

Anyone brought up in the Christian church can hardly miss the Christ and the cross images which emanate from this prototypical speech which might be given by a chief. Clearly, this center pole, the axis mundi of the Cheyenne tribal ritual is very similar to the Christian cross. But of course, the Cheyenne ceremonies are much more attentive to the earth.

I was thrilled one recent summer when Lawrence invited my husband and me to come observe the Concho Sun Dance, at least to see the center pole raised. He knew I was intrigued with that part of the event in which he participates.

We arrived on Friday evening after the people had already been in camp conducting various rituals during the week. Just outside El Reno, we followed our hand-drawn map, wending our way alongside the long drive lined by cedar trees, past the tribe's herd of grazing buffalo at the turnoff. We immediately saw the tepees and camp sites.

It was my first view of a modern-day Cheyenne camp—impressive in size and careful layout. I have read of course, of how the missionaries first went to the "camps" where the Cheyennes actually lived in community. The government officials spoke repeatedly of the Cheyennes' preference to live in camps in earlier years. Lawrence described his childhood spending time with his grandparents and other relatives at the camps. Thus this annual building of the camp is a reenactment of the ways of the traditional Cheyenne people. This camp we entered had been organized for the Sun Dance—the most important annual Cheyenne festival, the renewal of the earth—and also for a reunion, cooking fest, policy meeting, dance, prayer meeting, and feast!

I knew that the Chiefs' Day had already happened. Chief Hart explained that the chiefs had spent the day together talking about matters that matter. He referenced only one event they discussed—the upcoming trip of some twenty Cheyenne chiefs to Washington, D.C., to accompany Rick West, a Cheyenne native son and newly appointed peace chief and Director of the new Indian Museum of Art in Washington. The Cheyenne chiefs planned to walk with him in full regalia from the Washington Monument down the Mall into the new museum.

Lawrence was keen on this trip to Washington, I could see, as he mentioned, smiling, that they even talked of what to wear. Should they wear bonnets? Lawrence had never worn a bonnet, only using ceremonial feathers in his hair, but recently he had received at the Cheyenne Cultural Center a full-length chief's bonnet long kept by some non-native family in Hammon and now returned to the Cheyenne people. He wondered aloud whether he could have the cloth which holds the eagle feathers re-sewn in time for the event in Washington. The feathers, of course, were well-preserved over time.

It was a small question, but indicative, I realized, of Chief Hart's constant introspection about his role as a leader between two worlds. I immediately thought of a Cheyenne bonnet as a "war bonnet," and I wondered whether this was another matter of discernment for Lawrence. His life is a series of questions about symbolism, what is right, what is appropriate. I learned later that he did not wear the bonnet.

The Hart camp site was beautifully organized, facing south over open pasture from which I heard the coyotes howl later that evening. The children dashed off to play in the open pasture and returned to one of the tepees or tents. Three traditional tepees were set up, the closest one belonging to Lawrence's granddaughter; I saw her kneeling on a rug beside her bed, coloring. Her mother was busy cooking, for her husband's oldest son was "going in"—as an initiate in the ceremony.

Lawrence spoke of the evening's ceremonial activities. He wished that they could erect the heavy center pole before dark, because it is a difficult and dangerous task, and he worried that someone could be hurt in the dark. But the food had not been called for, nor had the women been called. It clearly had to happen after dark. Lawrence worried, but the schedule was out of his hands. The pledgers that year were in control of the schedule. The order of rituals must be followed. Chief Hart had already done his part, helping to choose the cottonwood tree for a center pole, taller and heavier than I had ever imagined. And he had chosen the site, directing the early construction which we saw as we arrived—a circle of smaller forked trees standing, ready to accept the center pole and rafter beams to become a lodge.

The ritual events would happen in their time during the evening and into the night. We sat in the shade at the Hart campsite and visited. Many were doing the same all around the camp, preparing, cooking, greeting, organizing. Grown Cheyenne children came in from across the country, many seen by local families only once a year, or as often as they are able to get away to attend the Sun Dance. Clearly, much of the weeklong event was about gathering, about food, and about visiting—checking in. I asked many questions, but the explanations were often lost on me.

Finally I recognized that people were involved in ritual behaviors. I did not want to break into the reverie. Also, I could see that this was about imbibing a ritual, understanding it in one's bones, because family members have been a part of the dance, a part of the prayer line, one of the women who slept in the lodge, one of the chiefs who advised, a sponsor. One must grow up with this ritual. The explanations were hollow. The meaning is in the doing; the meaning is in the being.

I recognized this when Lawrence came into camp to greet us. He was more effusive than usual. This was his setting. He smelled like smoke, and I told him that. He smiled, saying that he guessed it was a compliment. It was. Ritual is smell, and this was the smell of meat cooking, the smell of various kinds of fires, of various kinds of wood, of gas fuel and fire pits, every family's individually made fire and cooking rising up to join into a heavenly odor. For the young man in the Hart camp who was the night's initiate, this meal we were joining was his last meal before fasting. He ate first.

The soup was wonderful, filled as it was with a plenitude of beef. Salad. Rice with raisins. The food came out of large cooking pots, out of an amazing outdoor kitchen, fully equipped with sturdy furniture Lawrence had built and painted gray, adding a new piece each year, Betty told me. He was building his children's future in this camp, in this service. His eldest daughter, rather than his wife, was in charge, although Betty assisted and answered questions. I could see, however, that this time it was not Betty's event.

The Hart camp site does not use the old-fashioned willow arbors or shades I saw constructed at other places around the site, though both Lawrence and Betty noted that these structures are wonderfully cool places to retreat. The Hart site included at its center a wonderful covered dining room, kitchen, and sitting area. Much of this weekend, I soon saw, was about food and food offerings. Saturday morning I watched

Lawrence and Betty's eldest daughter Connie take out her computerized printout of the foods she needed to prepare at the Hart site. These were to be taken in and blessed and brought out along with the foods to be prepared at her husband's family's camp site adjacent. All the food would then eventually generate a huge feast on Sunday. Meanwhile, cars arrived and old friends greeted one another. There was work to be done—cooking, lodge preparations, painting of bodies, preparations for the evening's raising of the center pole, the lodge construction, singing and dancing.

Here is my favorite part. It is about being included, which I found was always the case when I was with Lawrence. Betty had told me to bring a prayer cloth, a strip of fabric the women bring to symbolize their prayers. My husband and I agreed as we drove to Oklahoma that we should pray for Rod Sawatzky, a dear friend suffering a brain tumor. Our gray-green strip of tie-dyed fabric was cut from a measure of cloth which I love, but it was pale beside their bright colors. After supper and after several calls for rituals related to food taken for blessing, the women at the Hart campsite began donning skirts over their shorts, shawls over their shoulders or heads, placing their prayer cloths over their shoulders, preparing to go into the central circle of the camp. They helped me to adjust mine. A little metal bucket was hung on the cloth of the mother of the newest Hart baby, Lexus. It was getting dark, and I could see in the distance, in the central area of camp, women beginning to form a line. I was allowed to join them with my prayer cloth.

It was for me a powerful, moving event. Maybe the growing darkness and the glowing campsites, the Oklahoma night air, and the smells from all around the central site created the kind of mystical experience I had that night. More likely, it simply felt wonderful to be included in a powerful ancient ritual. Sons or grandsons with flashlights walked old grandmothers carefully from their camp sites around the circle to the line forming for the delivery of prayer cloths. Then the men quietly disappeared. The women greeted each other warmly, taking hands in the dark. Many had covered heads, and the dark round silhouettes of women were beautifully female against the night sky and background fires. It felt like hundreds of us!

We stood waiting our turn in line, quietly visiting. The moment was not particularly solemn, but it was reverent. Ahead of us, women gave their prayer cloths to designated men to be tied to the fork of the center pole or to the other poles, all in some order and by designated persons, warrior societies, or chiefs.

When we had come to the center, a man held his arms out for us to drape our prayer cloths (Betty had told me to bring a length about two and one-half yards). Then we passed by a line of women sitting on the ground on bedrolls, whose hands we took. Some of them were old; one put her hands on Lexus' head and prayed in Cheyenne. Lexus' Grandmother Betty asked another to pray for her. We passed quietly in this line, with the kind of mystical hush I used to feel during Sunday evening services at Friedensfeld, my home church near Turpin, Oklahoma when we sang in closing, "Now the day is over. Night is drawing nigh." Shadows of the evening steal across the sky." The song always meant so much more than the words we were singing, placed us all in some reverie I could never articulate.

Each of the women we greeted would enter the lodge later that night. As we passed, each gently took my hands and looked at me, a greeting which felt like a blessing. They were sitting on the bedrolls on which they would sleep in the lodge, perhaps ten women, distinguished figures in this event. The power I felt came from their touch, the grace of such community elders praying, the community of women honored there.

Late into the night I sat on a lawn chair at a distance watching the ceremonies and rituals unfold. Things happened as if they were part of a theater production, in an organic way. The scene was dreamlike—many people, the smoke rising, the stars appearing, the hushed figures doing what they must do, the rituals progressing as if nudged by some higher power which asserted itself upon the players to perform their roles, take their places, follow some ancient instruction. I remembered Lawrence's repeated emphasis on preparations for ceremony, putting the pieces in place, obtaining the ritual elements. That instruction felt relevant here.

After all the prayer cloths were carefully transferred and tied to the center pole or to the poles placed in the cardinal directions, Chief Hart instructed a large group of strong young men as they rolled the center pole to the earthen hole prepared for it. They stopped to sing four times, then finally raised it carefully, fitting it into the hole prepared for the pole to stand upright. There was joy when the pole connected to the sky! The crowd shouted; the women lulued. It stood. Hallelujah!

Also difficult was the attempt to get the rafter poles, all adorned with willow branches and the prayer cloths, to fall into the fork at the top of the center pole. The men had to work hard to get the poles to fall into the fork, but finally the lodge was structured. Then, with careful ceremony, the fire was moved into the lodge, the buffalo skull was carried low along the ground by a woman in the ancient ceremonial way, and preparations were made to go inside for the dance.

Late in the night we left the site while dancing and preparations were still ongoing. We had a new appreciation for even this small part—one evening's observation—of the annual rituals of a Sun Dance we had been privileged to observe.

I love words. Words have always been my business. I am exasperated when I cannot find appropriate words—except in worship. In worship I am often happier with fewer words. There I long for silence and ritualized ways of being.

Douglas Comer discussed this necessary experience when talking about the ritual of the Sun Dance. He argued that "our bias in favor of words has now partly blinded us to the real impact of nonverbal communication. . . . It is *lived experience*, experience not limited to words, that conveys meaning. . . . And this is how ritual makes its effect" (1996, 70).

The Reverend Lawrence Hart spoke powerfully about tribal ritual in a manifesto he delivered to Native peoples at Native Assembly 2000 at the Hopi Reservation. His title was "Culture and Christianity." That address revealed him in his most prominent roles as peace chief, communicator, theologian, interpreter of the Scriptures, *connector*—earth to heaven, Mennonite to Cheyenne, Scripture to life.

When I listened to a recording of that address, I saw, perhaps for the first time, the other end of what I had heard that day years ago in his commencement address to a non-native audience. At the Hopi Reservation he spoke to a mostly Native audience who had questions about the use of tribal rituals. Must they give these up to become Christian? Clearly, he was addressing the tension between tribal rites and scriptural texts. The power of that address as I experienced it was Chief Hart's resounding admonition to his audience that the ancient tribal ways often reflected what has been lost by a whitewashed, Euro-Western interpretation of Scriptures. Such interpretations have lost the tribal rituals and the tribal Jesus. It was Hart's brilliant interpretation of his role in the Sun Dance that made his point.

In his address Hart explained that he served in two capacities for the Sun Dance. If needed, he performed the role of camp crier. In addition, he described his role as the one who cut the cottonwood tree. He explained that as camp crier he announced upcoming events repeatedly, facing in the Cheyenne cardinal directions. (He is third on the list of criers, he noted, and he was not called to that role the night I observed the Sun Dance events.) But before he can serve as a crier, he must undergo a specific ritual with an authorized traditional person. He must kneel on the ground, his arms out at length, and he must not look at the ritual itself.

Thus posed, he waits, head turned, eyes closed, while the traditional person spits toward his hands. He emphasized the word "spits" into the microphone, giving it its expectorant quality! As he told of this ritual, he acknowledged that his listeners probably imagined such spitting as "gross," offensive, pagan—not biblical or Christian. He demanded that his audience hold these judgmental thoughts and stay with him!

His second act of participation described in this address was cutting the tree that would become a center pole and which they would address as "grandfather." Again, he recognized the audience's reaction: perhaps his listeners thought of his participation here as pagan, the worshiping of trees, believing that inanimate objects became human.

Next, Hart turned to his biblical texts in his address. First, he explored Mark 8: 22-26, an account in which Jesus encountered a blind man the people brought to him, begging Jesus to touch him.

> He took the blind man by the hand and led him out of the village; and when he had put saliva on his eyes and laid his hands on him, he asked him, "Can you see anything?" And the man looked up and said, "I can see people, but they look like trees, walking." Then Jesus laid his hands on his eyes again; and he looked intently and his sight was restored, and he saw everything clearly. Then he sent him away to his home, saying, "Do not even go into the village."

As Hart interpreted it, Jesus spit on the blind man. The audience no doubt reacted differently, he noted, when they read the Scripture text than they did when they heard about the Cheyenne ritual. His point was that we can only see through the lenses we have, Euro-Western usually, not Native.

"I have come to the conclusion that the Euro-Western world has filtered out much of who Jesus is," Hart said. He noted that even Natives use these Euro-Western lenses to see Jesus. Hart argued that Jesus was a tribal person. Euro-Western people do not know what it is to be tribal. Jesus performed tribal rituals. He took the blind man out of town away from the village, a ritual proscription. Jesus used his saliva, a tribal prescription for blessing or healing, much as sage, sweet grass, or cedar might be prescribed in a Cheyenne healing ritual. Hart also cited the Isaiah 61 text which points to "oaks of righteousness" and the 1 Chronicles 16:33 passage in which trees are described as shouting out. The Scriptures too use the trees metaphorically for personified behaviors.

What Hart called for in this powerful message was a tribal view of Jesus. He acknowledged that the tribal ways of Jesus of the tribe of Judah were not necessarily equivalent to the tribal ways of the Cheyenne tribe. But Jesus was a tribal person, God's choice to reveal himself in a way that no teleevangelist in a luxurious sanctuary will ever understand, said Hart. He called up the image of the Jesus born in a manger in a barn, the Jesus with dust on his feet. This Jesus, Hart argued, was not Anglo. Tribal lenses for viewing him might have a better chance at seeing him for who he was.

Hart continued by comparing Judaic and Cheyenne ceremonies, like naming ceremonies, which he argued should be conducted in churches. He recognized the tribal rituals performed in a Jewish funeral—for example, those hired to wail for Lazarus—as no different from tribal rituals used by the Cheyennes today. Hart remembered that Jesus wasn't "fullblood," referring to the story of Ruth and Naomi in his lineage. "That doesn't matter!" he spit into the microphone with passion, talking now to Anglos who need a revelation. The Euro-Western view of Jesus would be much enriched by a tribal view of who he was.

Finally, Hart came again to the tribal view of the earth, as he did that day in his commencement address at Bethel College. This distinct expression of faith as seen by tribal peoples through their lenses must belong to the Christian tradition! It is a gift, Hart argued. He noted with deep regret that in the past half century both the Mennonite and Cheyenne peoples have evidenced increasing disregard for the earth, even though the two peoples once shared deep respect for this earth. We need to stay connected to the earth, he said. A tribal Christian view would incorporate the earth and all who live in it.

In the end, Reverend Hart even offered a Cheyenne tribal interpretation of the book of Revelation, that most controversial account of

John's vision quest. Hart believes that John in Revelation was saying that just as we use our God-given cultural tradition here on earth to worship, John's vision shows through his imagery the combined cultural traditions which will be used in heaven.

I sat silent alone in my office as I listened to Hart's impassioned voice on the audio recording of "Culture and Christianity." He had delivered this manifesto on behalf of a tribal view of Christianity. I sat a long time cherishing the experience of this sermon.

Then I remembered one of those moments I had with Lawrence I shall always treasure. We had spent several hours together as I conducted interviews during the day, but we agreed to meet again that evening after dinner. He wanted me to help him interview a candidate for a Mennonite Central Committee internship, someone who might be employed to help him in the major ongoing repatriation project he leads now. We agreed to meet later in the evening, even though it was at the end of a very long day for him.

It was dark as I made my way back along the sidewalks beside the sage smells, the variety of herbs which usher one into the Cheyenne Cultural Center where Chief Hart and the candidate were already talking as I arrived. The October night was hushed, the lights soft, the candidate telling of tours she had led at the Washita Battle Site. She said she did not go there alone at night. "You shouldn't," Lawrence told her. I wondered whether she was afraid of being confronted by the living in that place— or by the spirits of the dead.

Then Lawrence began to tell a story the way one tells a story he has not intended to tell—a story that does not come to consciousness until such a tired moment as this, when one no longer screens, and memory takes over. He remembered a "strange" event that happened to him when he was leading a tour to the Washita Battlefield Site. After their tour, he met with the group in a large room at the Coyote Hills Guest Ranch a short drive from the Washita site. There Lawrence had continued for the group his stories of the events that transpired on the Washita. One participant in his audience had brought her old Cheyenne mother to hear Lawrence tell these stories. At a certain point in the program, the old woman arose and made her way across the room to stand in the open doorway. Perhaps she had sat too long, or she might have just needed some air. As Lawrence finished with his presentation, he recalled, he decided to sing a song in Cheyenne. The song would conclude the program for that evening. As Lawrence now related the story, the mood was such that I dared not interrupt to ask what song he sang that night.

Lawrence continued then recounting what happened after he sang the song. As he stood at his place in the front of the room, visiting with the audience as individuals began to take their leave, the old woman came slowly toward him. "They were singing with you," she told him. "There, where I stood in the doorway I could clearly hear their voices in the night. They were singing with you." (I learned later from Chief Hart that the old woman was Rita Black, granddaughter of Jay Black, a former Arrow Keeper and direct descendant of Chief Black Kettle.)

I too have heard the voices of the old ones singing with and through Lawrence Hart. He brings their voices back from long lost times. He remembers their stories, their deeds, their words, and their ways of doing justice. He prays in the words of the old language, using the very phrasings which convey their understandings. He practices with care their traditions which preserve the tribal memory. He plucks their very bones from the forgotten shelves of history and restores them to the sacred ground of earth so that their spirits might sing once more.

EPILOGUE

I have a strong impulse to preserve the stories of the past—probably because I carry an ominous sense of the loss of my own family history. My paternal grandparents were dead before I was born. Because my maternal grandparents lived at a distance, I barely knew them. My father, with whom I was very close, died at age fifty-two before I was mature enough to trace the details of his fascinating life. I went to Lawrence initially to *preserve* his story.

When I began interviewing Lawrence in November 2002, I saw immediately that having been raised his first six years by his paternal grandparents, born in the early 1870s, had created for him a unique link to the Oklahoma Cheyenne oral tradition. Thus he was a generation closer to Cheyenne tribal ways than he should have been. His grandparents taught him to speak Cheyenne as his first language. They taught him to be Cheyenne in ways that his own parents could not have done. I wanted to preserve this historical link with his Cheyenne past. I value traditional ways.

Quickly Lawrence's journey became intertwined with my own. Though Lawrence is sixteen years older, many of his life experiences felt linked to mine. I share with him Oklahoma as my geographic taproot, the Mennonite faith history and stories, and Bethel College as alma mater. I would learn as I traced Lawrence's theology and recorded his values—that I share with him also a world view and belief system, though we were raised in different cultures.

Finally, from the day that I heard his commencement address at Bethel College, I became deeply interested in Lawrence's view of destiny, both his personal destiny and the destiny of a people or peoples. I wanted to seek out the source of his belief in divine movement which guides beyond mere coincidence. I have always believed that each of us creates our own destiny, and Lawrence's story reinforced that belief. Yet geography too is destiny—*place* defines us. I now recognize that one's destiny is also constructed by membership in a certain group or tribe, a sense of peoplehood, and the knowledge of one's people's ways.

I am guided in my telling of Lawrence's story by his interpretation of the events of history. He is guided by Cheyenne ways of seeing, albeit his memory is but one version of the truth. To be able to access in this story Lawrence's interpretation of history as he shared his journey and perspective was for me a gift of new understanding. Of course *I* chose the words to tell Lawrence's story, and this particular journey with Lawrence is my journey—one tells what one sees and follows one's own interests in the pursuit of another's story.

These intertwined stories—the stories of Lawrence Hart and and of Raylene Hinz-Penner, of the Cheyenne and Arapaho people and the Mennonite people in Oklahoma—are still being told. Others will tell these stories and tell them differently—perhaps because they will uncover additional past narratives, and most certainly because they will speak from their personal standpoints.

CHRONOLOGY

1700s—Cheyenne tribes located on Minnesota River and in what is today North Dakota

1820s—Cheyennes scattered from Missouri River to Arkansas River

1814-1864—Cheyennes located in Colorado along Arkansas

1834-1859—Bent's Fort Trading Era

1843—Afraid of Beavers (Lawrence Hart's great-grandfather) born

1864—Sand Creek Massacre

1864—Howling Water (Lawrence Hart's maternal grandfather) born

1867—Treaty of Medicine Lodge reserved Cheyennes land in Oklahoma and Kansas

1868—Custer's Seventh Cavalry attacked Black Kettle's village on the Washita

1869—Brinton Darlington, a Quaker, arrived in Indian Territory as Indian Agent

1871—John Peak Heart (Lawrence Hart's grandfather) born to Afraid of Beavers and Walking Woman.

1874—Battle of Adobe Walls in Texas

1875—Corn Stalk (Lawrence Hart's paternal grandmother) born

1879—Carlisle Indian Boarding School established in Pennsylvania

1880—First Mennonite Missionary S. S. Haury came to Darlington

1881—Mennonite Mission School opened at Darlington

1884—Chilocco Indian School established

1887—Dawes Act sold reservation land, set up allotment system

1890—Linguist Rodolphe Petter arrived, Darlington

1892—Allotments in the Oklahoma Territories taken by Cheyenne people in preparation for the 1892 land run.

1897—Homer Hart (Lawrence Hart's father) born

1898—Jennie Howling Water (Lawrence Hart's mother) born

1898—Mennonite mission work begun among Red Moon Cheyennes near Hammon

1901—Chief Red Moon died

1906—Chief Howling Water (Lawrence Hart's maternal grandfather) baptized by Rudolph Petter as first member of Hammon Mennonite Church

1916—Homer and Jennie Hart (Lawrence Hart's parents) married; seven children, 1917-35: Alvin, Lucy, Nora, Christine, Sam, Lawrence and Ramona

1918—Homer Hart began forty-year ministry in the Hammon Mennonite Church

1925—Chief Howling Water died

1927—Afraid of Beavers died

1933—February 24, Lawrence Hart born

1934—Betty (Bartel) Hart born, Hillsboro, Kansas

1936—John P. Hart became Cheyenne Chief

1952—Lawrence Hart graduated, Hammon High School

1952-1954—Lawrence Hart attended Bethel College before enlisting, Navy

1957—Lawrence Hart and Betty Bartel married

1954-1958—Lawrence Hart served in Navy and Marines

1958—Chief John P. Hart died
  Lawrence Hart became Cheyenne Peace Chief
  Jennie Hart died

1961—Lawrence Hart graduated Bethel College

1961-1963—Lawrence Hart attended Associated Mennonite Biblical Seminary, Elkhart, Indiana

1963—Lawrence and Betty Hart began service at Koinonia Mennonite Church

1968—Cheyenne Reenactment on Washita with Grandsons, Seventh Cavalry

1969—Lawrence Hart became Chairman of the Tribes for the fifteenth Business Committee

1977—Homer Hart died

1977—Cheyenne Cultural Center established

1993—Lawrence Hart appointed to the Review Committee for NAG-PRA

1996—Washita Battlefield National Historic Site established

1998—Lawrence Hart delivered commencement address at Bethel College

REFERENCES

Berthrong, Donald J. 1963. *The Southern Cheyennes.* Norman, Okla.: University of Oklahoma Press.

———. *The Cheyenne and Arapaho Ordeal: Reservation and Agency Life in the Indian Territory, 1875-1907.* Norman: University of Oklahoma Press.

Blackburn, Bob. 2004. Interview. Oklahoma Historical Society, Oklahoma City: March 24.

Chalfant, William Y. 1989. *Cheyennes and Horse Soldiers: The 1857 Expedition and the Battle of Solomon's Fork.* Norman: University of Oklahoma Press.

———. 1997. *Cheyennes at Dark Water Creek: The Last Fight of the Red River War.* Norman: University of Oklahoma Press.

"The Challenges and Limitations of Assimilation: Indian Board Schools." 2001. The Brown Quarterly 4 (Fall): 1-5. *www./brownvboard.org/brwnqurt/04-3/04-3a.htm* (accessed May 26, 2004).

Comer, Douglas C. 1996. *Ritual Ground: Bent's Old Fort, World Formation and the Annexation of the Southwest.* Berkeley: University of California Press.

Craighead, Sarah. 2004. "Innovative Concepts of Cultural Resource Management" in Harmon, David, Bruce M. Kilgore, and Gay E. Vietzke, eds. *Protecting Our Diverse Heritage: The Role of Parks, Protected Areas, and Cultural Sites.* (Proceedings of the 2003 George Wright Society/National Park Service Joint Conference.) Hancock, Michigan: The George Wright Society.

Ediger, Theodore A. and Vinnie Hoffman. 1955. "Some Reminiscences of the Battle of the Washita." *Chronicles of Oklahoma* 33 (Summer) : 137-141.

Friesen, Arthur and Viola Friesen. 1981. Unpublished notes of an introduction of Lawrence Hart, Reedley First Mennonite Church, October.

Good, Merle and Phyllis Pellman Good. 1998. *What Mennonites Are Thinking, 1998.* Intercourse, Pa.: Good Books.

Greene, Jerome A. 2004. *Washita: The U.S. Army and the Southern Cheyennes, 1867-1869.* Norman: University of Oklahoma Press.

Grinnell, George Bird. 1907. "Some Early Cheyenne Tales." *The Journal of American Folk-Lore* 20 (July September): 169-194.

Hart, Betty. Interview: June 17, 2003. Cheyenne Cultural Center: Clinton, Oklahoma.

———. Interview: October 20, 2004. Cheyenne Cultural Center: Clinton, Oklahoma.

Hart, Lawrence H. 1961. "Why the Doctrine of Nonresistance Has Failed to Appeal to the Cheyenne Indian." Research Paper for Social Science Seminar, 481, Bethel College, North Newton, Kansas: May 22.

———. 1967. "Statement before the Indian Affairs Subcommittee of the Senate Committee on Interior and Insular Affairs on S. 1933." Unpublished manuscript: August.

———. 1981. "Cheyenne Peace Traditions." *Mennonite Life*, 36 (June): 4-7.

———. 1992. "KAIROS: The Quincentennial Moment." *Mennonite Life* 47 (March) : 8-14.

———. 1996. "Testimony on Washita Battlefield National Historic Site Act of 1996 before the House Subcommittee on National Partks, Forest and Public Lands for H.B. 3099." Unpublished manuscript. July 25.

———. 1997. "Sand Creek and Oklahoma City: Constructing a Common Ground." *Mennonite Life* 52 (December): 33-37.

———. 1998. "Connections Past, Present, and Future." Bethel College Commencement Address, May 24, 1998. Unpublished manuscript.

———. 1999. "Legacies of the Massacre and Battle at the Washita." *Oklahoma Today* 49 (May/June): 59-63.

———. 2000. "Culture and Christianity." Audio Recording, Address to Native Ministries Conference. Mennonite Library and Archives, North Newton, Kansas.

————. 2000. "Lifeways of the People." Unpublished Address, Washita Symposium: November 17.

————. 2002. Interview. Cheyenne Cultural Center, Clinton, Oklahoma: November 12.

————. 2003. Interview. Cheyenne Cultural Center, Clinton, Oklahoma: March 5.

————. 2003. "Cheyenne Way of Peace and Justice: The Post Lewis and Clark Period to Oklahoma Statehood." *American Indian Law Review* 28 (30th Anniversary Reprint): May 27.

————. 2003. Interview. Cheyenne Cultural Center, Clinton, Oklahoma: June 17.

————. 2004. Interview. Cheyenne Cultural Center, Clinton, Oklahoma: March 23.

————. 2004. Interview. Cheyenne Cultural Center, Clinton, Oklahoma: October 21.

————. 2005. Interview. Bethel College Mantz Library, North Newton, Kansas: March 22.

————. 2005. Interview. Cheyenne Cultural Center, Clinton, Oklahoma: September 6.

Heinrichs, Don. 1985. "Jesus, Son of Wakan Tanka." Project Paper for History 770, "The Plains Indians," Kansas Heritage Center, Dodge City, Kansas: August 5-9.

Hoig, Stan. 1980. *The Peace Chiefs of the Cheyenne*. Norman: University of Oklahoma Press.

Hoig, Stan. 2000. *Fort Reno and the Indian Territory Frontier*. Fayetteville, Ark.: University of Arkansas Press.

Kliewer, H.J. n.d. "Hammon Mennonite Church: A Brief History." Mennonite Library and Archives, North Newton, Kan.: (SA II–544).

————. 1901. "Red Moon." *Cheyenne and Arapahoe Sword* 3 (November): n.p.

Kroeker, Marvin E. 1997. *Comanches and Mennonites on the Oklahoma Plains: A.J. and Magdalena Becker and the Post Oak Mission*. Hillsboro, Kan,: Kindred Productions.

Linscheid, G.A. 1935. "Brief Summary of Our Missionary Activity in Oklahoma." Unpublished paper: June 13, Canton, Oklahoma. Mennonite Library and Archives, Bethel College, North Newton, Kan.

Linscheid, Ruth C. 1959. "Henry J. Kliewer: A Pioneer Mennonite Missionary." Unpublished paper for Mennonite History, 351 at Bethel College: November 16. Mennonite Library and Archives, North Newton, Kansas.

Linscheid, Ruth C. 1973. *Red Moon*. Newton, Kan.: United Printing.

Llewellyn, Karl N. and E. Adamson Hoebel. 1941. *The Cheyenne Way: Conflict and Case Law in Primitive Jurisprudence*. Norman: University of Oklahoma Press.

Long Journey Home. 14-minute video by KOCO-TV. Oklahoma City, Oklahoma.

Lomawaima, K. Tsianina. 1994. *They Called It Prairie Light: The Story of Chilocco Indian School*. Lincoln: University of Nebraska Press.

Miller, Rachel B. 2001. "Cheyenne Cultural Center Staff Work to Pass on Language." *Mennonite Central Committee Communications*. August 16, *www.domino-18.prominic.com/A5584F/PressRelease.nsf* (accessed June 8, 2004).

Moore, John H. 1996. *The Cheyenne*. Cambridge, MA: Blackwell Publishers.

Pauls, Joleen Kaufman. 2004. *All Things Working for Good: Letters of a Young Man's African Journey*, Ed. Muriel T. Stackley. Hutchinson, Kan.: Pauls Publishing Company.

Petter, Rodolphe. n.d. *Reminiscences of Past Years in Mission Service Among the Cheyenne*. Self-published manuscript. Mennonite Library and Archives, Bethel College, North Newton, Kan.

Redekop, Calvin, ed. 2000. *Creation and the Environment: An Anabaptist Perspective on a Sustainable World*. Baltimore: The Johns Hopkins University Press.

Seger, J. H. 1882. "Historic Events." June 25. *www.historyoklahoma101.net/indian1882.htm* (accessed December 20, 2004).

Stewart, Omer C. 1987. *Peyote Religion: A History*. Norman: University of Oklahoma Press.

Viola, Herman J. 1998. *Warrior Artists: Historic Cheyenne and Kiowa Indian Ledger Art*. Washington, D.C.: National Georgraphic Society.

West, Elliott. 1998. *Contested Plains: Indians, Goldseekers, and the Rush to Colorado*. Lawrence, Kan.: University of Kansas Press.

THE INDEX

THE AUTHOR

Raylene Hinz-Penner was born and raised in southwest Kansas near Liberal, with extended family and emotional roots in central Oklahoma. She attended Bethel College in North Newton, Kansas, Kansas University in Lawrence and Wichita State University. For thirty years she lived in Newton, where she taught English at Bethel College for many years before moving to Topeka, Kansas, in 2003.

She has published poems, essays, and prison arts collections as well as giving many public readings and addresses concerning literature's impact on human life. She has special interest in the role of literature in building and nurturing community and bridging cultural boundaries; she has served as a scholar for the humanities, working on behalf of the Kansas Humanities Council. As a part of her interest in cross-cultural issues and "border themes," she teaches literature courses in prison arts programs.

Hinz-Penner is a lecturer in the English Department at Washburn University.